THE HUNGRIEST STARS

ALSO BY CAREY SALERNO

Tributary

Shelter

THE HUNGRIEST STARS

POEMS

CAREY SALERNO

A Karen & Michael Braziller Book
PERSEA BOOKS / NEW YORK

Persea Books, Inc.
90 Broad Street
New York, New York 10004

LIBRARY OF CONGRESS CONTROL NUMBER: 2025945784

Book design and composition by Rita Skingle
Typeset in Minion
Manufactured in the United States of America. Printed on acid-free paper.

TABLE OF ELEMENTS

∞

—AFTERGLOW—

Whatever it was I lost, whatever I wept for
Was a wild, gentle thing, the small dark eyes
Loving me in secret.

—JAMES WRIGHT, FROM "MILKWEED"

Sugar Season (Luger)

They weren't what I imagined, the woods dank with old water, too spoiled really,
if I'm being honest. And I want to be honest, especially with the woods. Woods, who are

supposed to be earnest and enveloping, like the ones of my childhood—*lovely, dark, and deep*—
which made easy magic of being a mile away from home where the survey tape strings spun

around the silver-gray scalped furrows of maple trunks like sprightly anklets, bouncing on
the frigid zephyrs, underneath my palm, were soaked through, threads sluicing the skin.

This is the call of the boundary: strands marking our trees and then our neighbor's. The ones
my German short-haired pointer knew not the difference between and was promptly shot

by the gun in the neighbor's hands. He'd warned us so he said. We should have
seen it coming when he called us to the woods, to heft our dead dog onto the blue tarp

we used to cover the split wood from rain, to drag him back to the space between the pony
shed and burned down barn. It was a hard winter rife with deer meat for dinner,

and damn that dog loved to run deer. And I get it. I do. Even as that's what ended him—
the feeling of sprinting through the dense forest rising all around, weaving between the trees,

the crisp scent of icy loam hanging below the mouth where your body becomes its own
thread that binds the woods together. The scent of deer hot in your nose. I know it well—

that lust, the tracing down to a clandestine bed far within the wild blackberries, softened by
the belly of our deepest wanting. And when I dream, I want to be Luger, that was his name

(His name the name of a gun, and was that fate, we could never say for sure, but the fact
never escaped me, that it was and feels important, that he was tied by name to violence,

and even before he died, to the unloving way in which the needles of the porcupine were
ripped from his nose and days after he bled and licked the blood from his face, wagging

what was left of his lopped off tail, part phantom limb that steadied his body), it's because I
dream of being more than just my body too, of the way he disappeared into the undulating

wheat. It was something to see: the blur of his liver roan physique, the pepper of his ticking
while he galloped, four legs airborne, gliding nearly, the beauty of his cadence,

and I'm crying thinking of how no one cried when he was killed, or when we buried him
angry, or when we walked into the woods to try to find where he died, where he crawled to,

belly on the ground, whimpering, sniffing for a spot to make tender, to soften with his
breath, the place where we would meet him beneath the luminous maple lines,

the ground beneath him gone cold but greening. His eyes open, an extinguished yellow. It
wasn't what we were expecting. It wasn't. And I want to be honest about that. I do.

The sky above us held no visible sun, just a density of ashy cloud, a fog from the ground to
the canopy. How alone we were out there, miles from any main street, miles

from any neighbors, except for marks between our land. Their trees and ours, as sugar
season, our own hungers, come to remind us.

Dandelions (The Adenomyosis)

What could embolden these lurking dendrites more than a belly corpulent with estrogenic
waves? In the overgrown, invaded garden, in my body, in the lawn expansive between the

road and the pale, rained-soaked house, I'm seeding tufted lesions of endometriosis,
spoiling them with gobs of caffeine, sugar, and every flit of scotch I serve neat, an

embarrassment of riches. And perhaps we all are as helpless against ourselves, our watch-
face-tapping, shallow graves, against our not so quiet habits, our covert versions of

homeostasis, our slow relent, unable as we are even to halt the toothed spears of the
dandelions, their glossy clustered fury, up early, when, like incited neurons they manifest

ablaze, taproots erect, smearing and sudden on the sleeping yard after so many months gone
dormant. I forgot how quickly the cycle can change is all. I forgot how at first, I'm all feet

and then it's just knees when the swells within me spatter the surfaces of what's being pulled
under, deprived of their oxygen the gasping muscles' clench deliriously back and forth, rain

funneling into their hollow roots, and the dandelions—to which I learned my anatomy is also
considerably averse, having rubbed the yellow blush-brush blooms on my face with friends

near the reservoir fence at ten, hoping to give the apples of our cheeks color like our idols
and minutes after we pressed the rosettes of sickly leaves on, my cheeks bloomed virulently,

swelling until my eyes sealed shut, the white blood cells and macrophages gluing membranes
together—were flowers I couldn't see for days when they finally started to appear, when

even then my body was arranging for this rhythm, my parents wetting a washcloth and
pressing it to my face to dissolve my mistake, and like them, there's so much I want to rake

clear. Even after this long while, even after the skin has become too raw to touch, even after
every year, the dandelions somehow multiply their glut, spreading indignant from the

neighbor's yard to ours and then from ours to everyone else's, like at first how the rogue
blood started spilling from the notched uterus, then the ovary, and when its path ruled

unfettered, progressed exultantly onto the colon and liver, kidney and stomach, even the salmon pink lungs. Now the muscles. Their surfaces peppered, and when the shoots of the

dandelion pierce through the crabgrass, the ryegrass, the dead grass, you know you're in trouble but even so this kind of trouble is somehow always the hardest to see coming, its

dazzling acid, its yellow not yet fully blossomed, biting, sour, the sharp ends of the grooved petals wholly unformed, dour, a gentle containable thing, the deceit of the dandelion

coupling with your hope that the flowers might pass you by this season until one by one they begin to loudly multiply, to unfurl, and then suddenly every lawn is their wasteland, the body

a wasteland too. You want to mow it all down so low the blades dig back the earth, till the topsoil, dry it out and start again, erase the black of your organs, you want to pull from the

lawn all the dandelions you can before your eyes swell shut, you want to swallow all the heads of the drugs to make you limp and compliant, hoverfly gone crazy, belly distended,

stupor dulling it to the pain inflicted by dandelions, by adenomyosis, but isn't it's better to make your peace with such persistence? Better to live skidding over rutted remedy than

to be plucking at the relentless stems that keep popping. (Just take the drugs religiously already, hon.) How many times can you mow the yard in a week without the neighbors

beginning to wonder if you are really just that mad? Pollen drunk. Obsessing-just-a-*little*-bit-bitch. And the dandelions, too, know they have you beat. From the day the first one in the

grass—its seed having flown from the lips of a girl who dipped her bike into the lawn to puff the white kernels of a blowbell, tendrils twirling through the air and delving into the earth

(She seemed happy enough at the time. Why spoil things for her?), the seeds burrowing, consecrated with a kiss which was also the permission granted to stay, to bloom and thrive

and propagate—you could never have known what you were born with: the wet interior, plentiful blood overturning to nourish the lesions, nurture their network in the tissues that

jam the muscles, seal off the labor of the organs. One day they'll get inside those too—not a
threat but a promise—the same girl will clip the squelchy stems from a ball-shaped patch and

carry them over the threshold into each house, so many dandelions tight in her fist. She'll
place them in a jar and provide them water, her desire to accumulate something outweighing

any other, her lips painted red, falsies on her lashes like all the girls wear now, she'll watch
your eyes water, allergic, when you tell her thank you. You tell her how beautiful,

withdrawing into your drink, you're not crying, not yet, muttering about how gorgeous
and sharp within you the tendrils leeching, the radiant and bitter blooms.

The Fulguration (In Vitro Fertilization)

I wanted lightning to make upon me its best version of hypervelocitic impact,   so I went to
the field where lightning has been known to gather, so I was told, where the   keraunic
measure reported is well above average according to every saccharine   declaration,
scaled to the top of the undulate sand where around me was poured   all its spun sugar, its
dry dune where nothing grew upon any surface, sucrose worth   less than nothing, high
as the dunes were, sweeping even, and the only hint of   vegetation was the
slumbering windbreak cottonwoods, their enormous   subterranean trunks frozen
hundreds of feet into the damp grains below the   imminent storm's sudden updrafts
that were sifting through the beckoning fans of   their flirty branches which overhung
the buff parabolas of the sand shells like   arms, nearly begging for any trickle of
light, for a bird for a millisecond on   any single branch, to be taken from the misery of
their sluggish, smothering deaths,   to, let's be clear, be touched; interred as they've
remained, and the lightning   when it finally came splintering the sand, cutting its
path—they took it, will   accept what they're given, in no position to be choosing, how
the impact casts a   fossilized version of itself, that when submerged in particles of
iron and silicone   and everything else cools more quickly than we'd imagine lightning
ever might,   preserving the shape of its strike, the field of study called paleolightning
used to   determine the signature of fulgurites, the number, pattern, the frequency,
which   like bruising, has been deemed a workable unit of measure

|
|
|

as far as embryo   freezing is concerned, as much is known
about as much as we can know it, as much about how   and when lightning strikes as about
windshear and microbursts, I mean, the science   is improving, is surpassing the
fundamental, and those interested in amassing   new data find there's money to be had,
and, too, that there's a testable limit to every   reported accuracy, according to the doctor
in front of us who insists the slow-freezing   cryopreservation method employed by his
clinic on our embryos is *just fine*. We have our   doubts and it's his job to quell them, to
make us believe in how we might lie down in   a nightblue field and be struck by the first
bolt of lightning loosened beneath the frost-   frenzied virga, its strong indication of
looming violent downdrafts accumulating   above us, and even when we say how hard
we've tried already—that we might yet collapse   in our bed and manifest something as
impressive, as seemingly interstellar

|
|
|

the frequency by which lightning strikes any given
surface, and perhaps, by extension, like   other probabilities, like the more fulgurite
in your pocket, the higher the likelihood to get what   you want if you want something, if
you can carry the fulgurite away from its field, if you can   dig it up without breaking it,
if they let you leave the premises with all that vitrified silicone   weighing down your
khakis the way it does, bulging, obvious, to later lay at the feet of the   altars of your
pushy, greedy gods whoever they are, if they'll even accept what you're   offering,
picky as they've become, if the mob of you can settle down enough to   meditate over
these gifts, to conjure something forth that's more than chance, to   polish smooth
between your thumbs and palms just like all the reasons that   brought you to this field
in the first place, to see if you truly feel like living (and do   you?), wearing them,
rubbing them into your skin like oil, like ink, this very   dune the surface of obligation and
everything that's beneath its rind barren, its   powdery atmosphere somehow still
sucking you up and into itself—updraft,   downdraft, say it's forever—you saying you
believe when you can't see the hard truth   of never

|
|
|

into where we've had   enough with ice crystals, even at these low
altitudes, and there's no getting to "the top of"   a thunderstorm no matter how high you
set your sights, yes, the crystals dripping onto the   frozen soil are pretty enough but . . . it's
enough already with being pretty, it's up to here   with the beginner's glass-making, he came
to work drunk, his tissues saturated, his lips loose,   everything permeable, he sang bold songs
and the words quickly trailed off into wet   mumbling, with half the embryos melting
before they completely thawed, the water   inside of them seeping from the seams of
their membranes when the intracellular icicles   microsliced them open, slopping every
precious metal, when they lay deflated, then   dried upon the agar of the dish upon his
attempted collection, hands unsteady, icicles   like the ones only pretty to the little child
who spots them suspended from the edge   of the roof of the winter house, referring
with mittened hand for everyone else who   understands better, knows that the

lustrous pendants dribbling are but one thing:
repair it, but since there's no fixing microtears
our embryos turned hard in seconds, vitrified.
dangerous at freezing due to the sheer volume
happy to succumb on the sand while it flashes
accrescent heat, where the retrieval table reclines
knees and await the next doctor's jolt

a warning; trouble awaiting your hand to
in the furring of a mitochondria, we'll have
We've seen what lightning can do, most
of water rephasing at this level, and we're
the full length of its legs at us in the
us back to prone, where we spread our

|
|
|

and we love a solid glamour, but looking
at each other, there is none; instead we're   only petrified like the minerals of sand
transmuted by fulguration, all we feel in   its place is the depth of the duplicities we've
piled sand to cover even when at first   it all blew away, hard labor, packed tightly like the
cottonwood whose roots reach too   far deep into the dune to ever resurface (we all
make mistakes), to be heard even,   to ever know the world again as maybe it did, to ever be
excavated, to ever have the   opportunity to feel the rush, the transformation that
overcomes the air when   finally the storm sets in, when the first rains fall, black on black,
overserved clouds   finally rolling up, should not have driven, twists purling coolly on
our scalp, in our   branches, everything standing straight on its end, against our leaves
whipping, gusts   up into our faces regardless of invitation and sticks sand to our lips,
lack of boundaries   welcome, making the stable flies around us, too, mad, sting as if
their lives depend upon   it and maybe they depend upon it, as ours depend upon
forgetting, the storm   forgetting's harbinger (what did it do last night?), how we
realize we've wasted our short   lives now they might be over, having forgotten to devour
what we can while we could,   whoops, too late, no hunger left for preserving, as a
way of protecting the self from rain,   from lightning, which if it comes for you, you are
already part of it before you know,   vitrified like the embryos, and we'll take the
massing streaks of water that   appear as if being sucked back into the clouds slouching
above straws loose in   their mouths instead. We'll rely on rain to make us wet. We'll
leave with our   chart, its hundred loose leaves of copy paper graceless, flapping in
the parking lot.

|
|
|

its shadows you laid down in during the rain-
where you heard your name being called and
storm, disobedient, dog, the hysteria of the tone
wind snapping against the trees you thought
one in the same, and all the sweeping rye and
face smelling like blood orange and jasmine &
the field already long emptied of trees, sending
invitation for lightning only, if you'll just accept,
wishes to refuse what shelter's offered them,
fed in lieu of steady rain upon their foreheads or
the earthworms are beginning to rise from
flooded, teemed to the surface, a consolation
having been poured past their brims with
primed to be plucked by the mouths of
enough, when they descend on newly oiled
that kept them a restless dry, preening beneath
tucked in at their sides, obedient until it was
them were only hardly quivering, aftershocked,
curling up toward the clearing sky which was

and then later to the night meadow,
storm and let everything cover you in itself
couldn't move, wouldn't come in from the
of the cry whirling into the sound of the
might fall any minute into you, becoming
brazen sweet pea hovering over your wet
rose, everything you wanted to devour but
you its best, sending you its regrets, a flat
a flat invitation for anyone, too, who
to refuse what protection might be force-
to pressing cheeks to the wet dirt wherein
their beds like buoys having already been
at best, having been fattened and readied,
water, membranes permeable as they are,
ready grackles when the storm eases just
wings from the trees that refused to fall,
their blackened canopies, that kept wings
time, until they knew that the leaves above
glossed in rainwater drying and then finally
their cue to dive

|
|
|

where we were, lying,
wriggling, ready to be bullied, despising   the lightning for not having done its job, which
it seemed from afar to be so very good at,   but nothing ever performs live the way it's
caught on tape, fact vs. after-the-fact, the production   value of pornography let's call it,
and we'll leave a bad review now, since we overhear it's   struck more than something
else nearby: a house for one, a man who tried to save himself   but was flung by its
powerline blast into a nearby cast of jewelweed, the high voltage   producing dazzlingly
lechatelierites—a fulgurite of copper, and a sedan whose passenger was   saved by the
grounding tires, rubber only melting on the asphalt, who didn't   become fulgurite, whose
body was missed, too, by the grackle as it narrowed its gaze   on the fat jelly tubes slowly
arching through the grass, eye between the writhing and   the blades discerning, between
the sky and the ground where they smash against   the meadow floor, where our
breath is both air and dirt with a cheek against it,   a desire to flee upon both, a desire to
stay within both, as a perfectly still, as an   inbetweenness, as a desire for something
sudden to rip us away, no bird big enough   for that I'm afraid, no luck either, as much as
you would roam the interminable sand,   as much as you nip your knuckles between the
white of your front teeth, leaving   little marks, bruises only surface level, bland, they
too eventually disappear

|
|
|

We could use
some luck. We could stand to get lucky.   We have the embryos kept on liquid
nitrogen, kept in the silvery fog of the freezer,   vapor pouring on the lab tech's feet when
the dewar unlocks, cinematic, embryos unlike   the brittle glass of melted silicone driven
deep into the sand, which if you try to unearth   crumbles in your hand, we understand the
process to bring forth atypical elements is   complex, the flash act hardening
everyone's resolve to create bloodlines in   the field made of agar, its little crop circle,
its cultivator who injected the eggs with a   micropipette, intracytoplasmic, one at a
time, then feeding them everything sweet and   water fat, every raw mineral like that, like

the ones the lightning dries to glass—petrifies,   lines with effervescences, and if fulgurites are so
fragile, what does that say about   the enduring power of lightning? Of us?
We, too, are as petrified. We, too, transformed   by every storm descending, a hard breath
over the petri dish, by every retrieval of eggs,   every retrieval of glass sudden in our
hands, the coarseness of hollow tubes, their   glassy interiors like wet eyes when we fail
to keep our shit together, when the blastocysts   expire again, and again at the speed at
which is not unlike how the summer storms   barge through the doors looking for
another fight, their silverly bolts missing us   where we stand in the field of the
insufferable protection of dune, feel their low   soil fertility, try
to feel alight

|
|
|

and consider what might happen, as much as   you might wish for fulgurite to be fulgurite
or to shatter, due to crushing, to transform   into something wholly other than yourself
by the suddenness of the act (maybe,   we've seen it before), of smashing with purpose,
of being handled with little care,   and here again, the feelings arise—what would yank
you from where the cottonwoods   thirst an overwhelming thirst, the lack too much for you,
where mere drops of water make   it to their clustered trunks if they're lucky, if fortune is
on their side, if fortune even exists   that far beneath the ground, buried by sand as is
every ring of every tree, as was the trees'   certain sweetness, its question, unascertainable,
knowable only to the blackout trunks   interred there too, cloning their roots in the
dark, incarnate in their absolute isolation, in   their numbering of years, their leaves
chattering in the wind and it's the best they can   hope for when the storm moves in,
runs its hands over the gale-blackened lake, for   certainly they too could someday
be fulgurite, couldn't they? Is there a classification for   that? They too, like we, want
transformation, tongues crashing soaked against our skin,   would try every high
frequency field just to say they touched lightning even   if after they could only say
nothing at all, stupefied by the splendor of it, of having   been rephased, made smutty,
made sweet, a lasting paradise within each, the earth,   a comingled element beneath the
sand, where that new galaxy expands

The Manatees (The Snowstorm)

We could just let such griefs overtake us, let the way they seep into our morning news feeds—
the little losings of each other we do every morning, pushing back the dreamy stupor—

stop us from seeing the finer contour of the shore that delivers the dazzling bay. We could
let such griefs spill back through our fingers, back into this larger body of invisible living

where below the surface the manatees float above their algal beds like sunken buoys. And
perhaps they are still soundly sleeping. And when I lean over the rail to tell them . . . I mean,

god, anything, they sink their pink bodies further down into the bay's winter garden, its
seagrass, its water hyacinth to the fluff of water celery and alligator weed and horsetail

paspalum, what I can't see below. I know it's there. I mean, of course, beauty is probably
only skin deep but the turquoise face of the water isn't all that beautiful without

the hope of the impossible bodies of the manatees ballooning to disturb its surface.
What I'm saying is I want to know that something rests beneath our surfaces too.

I want to know that heartaches also happen underwater, in the places we swim to at
night or maybe in the middle of the day, dreaming at our winter desks. It was less of a

whisper and more of a petition when I said it: all I see are the jellyfish swarming.
Everything is so unclear. And, too, it was much less than what I wanted, which

I think is just about what we probably can expect to receive. As in on the other end
of the phone line was the news you are back in the hospital, that you hadn't slept for days,

that you just sat smoking at the window waiting for something, waiting for something. I had
to step out of the restaurant to hear it. And what can I do that I haven't already

except the senseless things you showed me early on were acts of love, by which I mean
something like driving through a blizzard with my headlights off in order to find you

stranded in the eye of it, lightless and windblown, run off the road snow wetting your face.
What else when the whiteout doesn't end. The things I wasn't taught I don't know.

Like how to sink down into the mush of the seabed before the storm arrives, how to nestle
my body into the thick of its grass where the bright greens blacken and your voice

transforms into a steady hum, a muffled heartbeat, so close to the bottom now,
away from the heat of your chest, I stick my hands into the frozen mud to steady myself.

It's cold but not the way the iced cornfield glistens against the frost, glazing the red mouth
of the barn pink, its doors left sweeping, the racoons all huddled together inside.

And I'm not a gaze animal—another thing you taught me. I don't eat what you eat,
forage what you forage, sleep when you sleep in the rotting hay above the horses.

I read the news, wholly unbeautiful, and feel its grimness seeping at my edges
like the dye from a wet book jacket. I shake my coat before I put on my clothing for the day.

I feel the want pull me to the water's edge. I say it to the manatees and the manatees
reply with their nothing.

The Snow Fountain Weeping Cherry (Little White Dreams)

It was kind of like a peripheral haunting when the snow fountain started to bloom—so many
little ghosts popping up just beyond the front picture window, blossoms heavy with frost.

Planted in the shade, the cherry had to get on with its flowers at some point. And the
neighbor's magnolia, too, starting to bud, soon will be *shitting flowers* all over her car, I kid you

not is what she said to me when I told her I wanted one for myself. *I guess if you're into that
kind of thing*, she muttered slamming the screen door as she went inside for more margarita.

We're not really friends. And inside me too, the rusty bells at the edge of my hip are clanging
together, waking us with their obnoxious blaring in the middle of the night, calling me to the

window, as if I'm late to church, to see what the little apparitions of a sobbing tree are doing
now, to breathe *into the space* like the ayurvedic masseuse taught me, pressing her palms in

rhythmic circles over my abdomen, and in times like this I really wish that *she* wasn't so full of
shit, that something actually halted hard metal on its pendulous track, the blossoms from

falling on mid-size SUVs. In the night's long shadow, everyone else in the house sleeps
deeply, even my dogs. They don't stir when I rustle out of the sheets, not even a knowing

look, and who can say I'm not just another ghost out of time, full to the brim with buds
who are thirsty to be flowers? Maybe the mechanic across the street, up with his new

shepherd, who is also gazing out his front window trying to catch the furthest point afield
on which to focus, employing any proffered methodology at all to subdue the desire, its lures

dangling their very front of sleep, little white dreams panting against his neck, understands.
I'm not alone even when I'm alone. And I don't think the weeping cherry's snow fountain is

billowingly glacial but rather is likewise powerless, too, to fantasize its own fantasy, cascading
in a place it's said to be between joy and sadness, a bell's clapper frozen to its gaping mouth.

Certainly, its name is a tongueful and that must get so tiring along with how it roots bore
relentlessly, clawing closer to the organ meat of our house. How long can this go on?

Still, before they rust, the cherry's flowers are so briefly immaculate, the tender pink of the
very inside of them, blushing where they take hold of the branches that hang like ready

switches, leaving me glamoured, while the ovary stirs in its old bird's nest. If they were
awake, my dogs would remind me nothing can ferry us back to the same field we vanquished

in our dream, a reminder I could use when concentrating on the nevercherries while the next
spell of pain runs its course, the purity of pink bronzes on the old sheets of every petal,

and further afield forsythia glow like thousandfold apparitions against the persistent dark,
wherein the man across the road is returned beneath his comforter blessedly, pup curled at

his feet; they're nodding off, the havoc of the neighbor's magnolia only beginning to unfold.

The Binaries

X-Ray

Whether from the star's act of playing the counterpart or it being assumed counterpart to various acts of being, we consider the significance of—what's dispatched between the binaries, their unwilful compromise, their foreverness of tit for tat—an abundance of lithe matter precipitating from the raw mouth of the *collapsed* into the reluctant mouth of the *normal*, producing that which calls for further analysis, an expert to push silver printed films onto the wall-mounted lightbox and interpret the exact intention, each connotation, the accretion disk of edematous desire. As in there is a funnel point through which hydrogen and helium are persistently messengered. As in there must be a mediator present to elucidate the potential for innumerable misinterpretations, a material intervening, to record the right and wrong of the exchange in the little book that stays in the junk drawer of the kitchen. As in sometimes what's created is a disputable pulsing while at others the acts are demonstrably thermonuclear. As in keep your voice down so the neighbors won't hear. As in please stop leaving every goddamn light on in this house. As in the lusters of the stars blip and need time to recover, if they can recover, on their own. As in don't say another word to them right now.

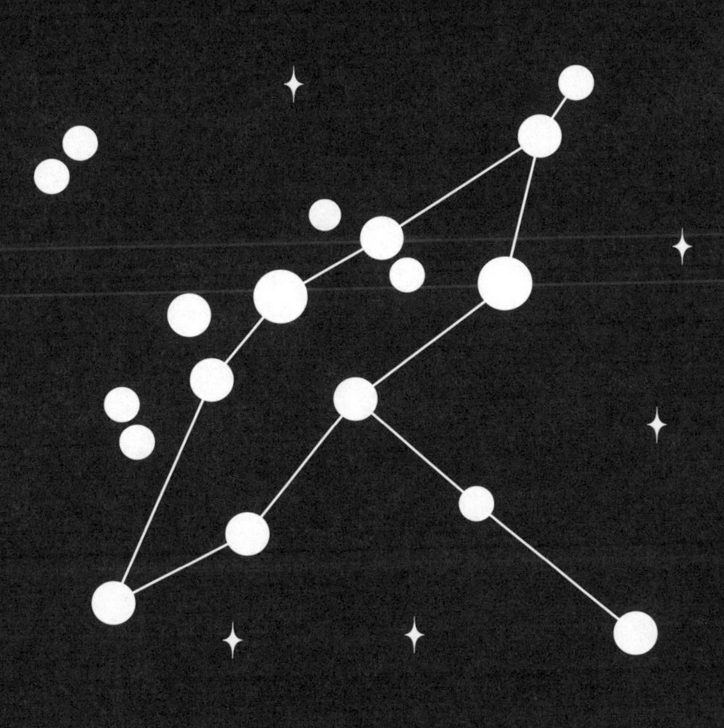

Gardens of Paradise (Eden Anamnesis)

I didn't believe in paradise standing at the alter which was high ground between two planted evergreens, a florist officiating.

But I did believe in the idea of paradise. That I wanted paradise. I believed in my capabilities.

I could make paradise.
I said yes to the work.

Paradise: a walled garden where animals and flowers can walk among the humans in something called peace which is another word for control, as in the control line showed but not anything else. No matter how hard I squinted at the test. Blank like the feeling of walking through a tame garden–the orangery–on a hot day in Versailles.

that the patient had a shall

was poor and cavity visualization was poor.

only filled and spilled.

Attention was turned to the right
was again allowed to fall

until all disease was removed on

some bleeding along the excision site

The ovaries were free
›d quite normal at this point.

This was also secondary to a uterus that was fairly fixed

Red river paradise after the red lines of paradise on the test that tested whether one would be granted entrance to paradise. Paradise in the hotel room high above the lower east side, at the bottom of a glass of topped off gin, paradise's seeping stemmed by an entire box of tampons, by bottle service in the subterranean nightclub, by floor to ceiling windows in the shower stall.

The hydrangea wouldn't grow, the shrub that smelled like honey what was it, the gerbera daisies and the azaleas. The lamb's ear, the hostas, the balloon flower bells you imagine are bluer than any eye from your past. You'll never know what paradise would have looked like—stop daydreaming. The iris. The stargazer lily. The hellebore and lilac. The peony, so pathetically dazzling. Its heavy head hanging from its delicate neck in paradise. We think thoughts that are the roses, more thorns than anything else.

When we hired experts, they made a lot of guesses look like answers. No upspeaking women were permitted to set the work back. The tubes were canulated while we were sleeping. The balloons inflated and placed to hold the garden of the uterus in place, to keep the garden open, propping the gate, rusted iron as it is, sewed shut by the congealing rain, the wind, the sun. These elements will indeed ruin a garden

we are told.

Vials and sharps containers: I'm pretty sure they didn't make it to paradise. I'm pretty sure they're officially excluded. Too many on the invite list already, they'll have to sit on the other side of the gate. They'll have to get crafty and build a horse, something far less red, something with fewer plastics, less jangle. In paradise, no one wants them. No one wants to acknowledge they exist, that with them, you exist.

inside the uterus, the balloon elevated, the distal catheter was tied
instrument counts, sponge counts, and needle counts were correct|

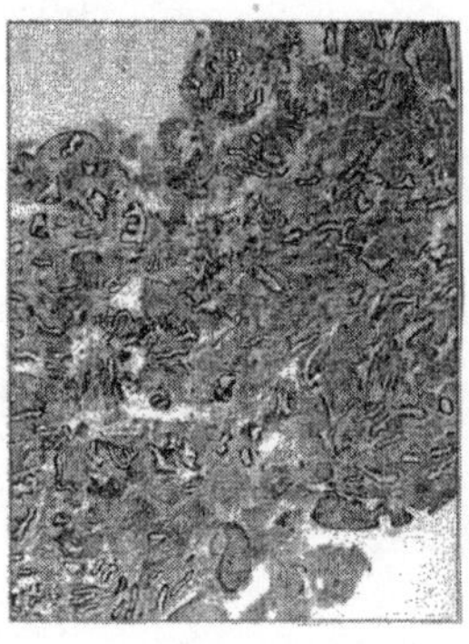

Salmon

blueberries

spinach

eggs.

The foods of paradise.

Just ask paradise.

Ask literally

any paradise.

There's a quadrant in the garden where not even a dandelion would be caught dead. Where the experts claimed they could wash its earth down with hormones, pushed by syringes into the soft bellies of the ground, as it were. They could bring what's been broken back to life, flood what's arid, what cracked within in, cure the hostile environment you've grown all your life. It takes money and time. How much? Depends on the garden. Depends on how much money you have, how much time. First, let me ask, how hard do you want to see a few blowbells?

At the bottom of a bottle. At the bottom of several bottles. Paradise. No paradise. Did we find it? Are we too drunk to say? Admit you want it too. More bottles. More worms. More salt. More honey. More nectar. We'll catch it somewhere. Paradise can't have gone far.

Paradise between my legs
Paradise anywhere but our bed
In our friend's bathroom during a dinner party

I'm not afraid. In paradise
I know how to hold my tongue,
how not to startle the peacock,
the sleeping deer

and the patient was draped in a sterile manner.
was examined and was untouched.
but this was still well away from
carefully superficially excised
it was untouched.
Superficial
The patient
the anterior superior iliac spine
was replaced
was performed
Using the laser at that setting, attention test fired outside the abdomen with a good aiming beam.
It was
so a current, opened until it was flush with both
its course to be identified all the way down
from the left
carefully taken down from the left.
carefully elevated and taken down medially to free the
canal.
under visualization
she was returned to the recovery room in stable condition.

It was clear my haven was less curated than we'd hoped. Whose fault is that? Whose fault is it for mistaking the lion for a sheep? Whose fault the snake for the squirrel? What feeds into itself inside of us at night, eating its own tail, isn't found in the wilderness.

Who would send me to plant the garden? Someone so unwise. Garden full of corpse flowers. Wretched in their towersome beauty. Garden full of deadhead and empty stems. Garden overgrown and tangled. Garden upside-down and acrobatic. Too much work even for the monkeys we imported, for the rats too, a lot of work.

Transformed, paradise into failure. Pleasure into we don't know exactly what, a reminder of what's suddenly ragged, what suddenly is devoid of its radiance, its gorgeousness brimming. Nobody wants it now. There's no praise for what doesn't work, but don't misunderstand: we have words. We say what we like and paradise hears us. Paradise laughs to itself and wonders if it was just a joke. We can't be serious, paradise thinks.

Paradise is a garden getting too far away from itself. Paradise is the secret garden within the obvious garden, the one you plant in the dark when everyone is fast sleeping, the one accessed by skeleton key, by ten-digit passcode, by the way the moonlight hits the icy marble and casts an exact shadow of its object as a decodable pattern across the groomed shrubbery. If you have a cipher. Do you have a cipher?

I can still be beautiful.

WITHOUT AND WITH CONTRAST
There is retroverted uterus.
There is diffuse thickening
mild mural finger-like enhancement
another fibroid vs. part of adenomyosis.
The uterus is bivalved to reveal a pyramidal uterine cavity
less likely an endometrioma.
PROBABLE CONTAMINATION.
__platypoloid__

You get what you pay for in paradise
The best gardens are really all money
Ask anyone with money

My friends report back that they fucked in the Orangery on our school trip to Versailles, but when I saw the garden, I couldn't see how it was probable. The landscape so stripped. The trees were lollipops pierced into the ground. Their fruits picked bare. There wasn't any wildness within which to hide. Nothing to smear the body. Nothing bruised on the ground. Just clean gray gravel on the endless dry walkways through the garden empty of gardens. The rich garden too rich for sex—better a Petri dish for your elements to mix, better yet the back room of a chemistry lab
where you can play with fire. But!
No fires in paradise, please.

Paradise we thought we knew you and here you are: a stranger still. Going a little madder even each year. Hanging vines covering the only way out. If we made this paradise, certainly we can forget how to find each other in it? Certainly, paradise will understand being paradise, being the paradise we built for itself, the paradise of endless labyrinthian alleyways. The gardens after all made from the shameless labors of youth, so many muscles that can work long days, hands that knew everything except how to know better.

What we manicured. What we cut away. What we forgot to tell each other. What we only told ourselves alone in our downy beds, the night air descending a lot more like a fisher's call than we'd hoped. I don't think I can remember it now. That bloodcurdling refrain. Enough to try—I don't think I care.

carefully identify those bleeding vessels and desiccate them until there was complete hemostasis.

NEGATIVE
NORMAL
NEGATIVE
NORMAL
NEGATIVE
NEGATIVE

The information herein is intended only for the entity to which it is addressed

We test the soil in paradise. We test it again. Sometimes twice a week we test it. The nurses tie a tourniquet and slap the arms hard at 7am. They draw the blood and make polite conversation, something that tries to distract us from how fucked paradise is, how fucked we are when there's no fucking at all.

Herb	tropical	water
botanical	green	wall
zen	floating	enchanted
hanging	frozen	formal
rock	sensory:	

these are all types of garden.
Magnificent as they are.

They are not paradise.

Into the fluffy bed of the garden, we try to guide the precious seeds to take their places. The experts practice. The novices push needles into oranges, then into the land just outside the garden, the paradisian envelope, imbruing the soil. It turns blue and purple, a sickly yellow green. You're doing it right, says the expert, syringe in hand. Count back from ten. You make it to four when the needle goes in.

Paradise: your face in the mirror
Paradise: your row of perfectly white teeth gleaming at me in the dark
Paradise: the drunks showering
Paradise: the pond full of fish fat and ready for more elixir
Paradise: the refusal of the fish to move from the shade, the cool water love of grave dreaming

and Continued? excised

to low signal area seen in

complex cystic lesion
corresponding to the complex

suggestive of an ovarian neoplasm,

focus
There

Tissue diagnosis is suggested.

body, likely representing which may represent another

Contact us immediately

destroy the document.

Are you death or paradise? The deer lying down with the goose. The goose alone in the fountain gloaming. To be fair, they're both taking things hard and so are we. All the water we pumped in to keep this garden going, to keep what's beyond the wall from us. To preserve the lush green against our parched tongues. So, it's thirst we settled on. And thirst is—well, thirst is heartless.

There are many thanks in paradise. There are many call you laters. There's a lot of attention to detail, experts on the case monitoring the level of chemicals. We need it just right. One more month and it could be paradise, they say. Like hummingbirds drawing nectar from the depths of the coves of foxgloves. Hi, it's patient 2282 calling, and I was just wondering, I forgot to ask earlier, did we remember to plant the foxglove?

Paradise: your mouth on my thigh
Paradise: my thighs beneath the gown I tied at my side
Paradise: the prayer said with a hand over my abdomen, with a hand releasing the embryos into the garden that was my level best

In paradise we know that turtles bask under the cover of darkness. They bask on the backs of crocodiles. They bask on the tips of trees felled by wind and rain. They cool their bodies against the zephyrs of the night air. They pile onto one another and when they've had their fill of this closeness, they slip back beneath the blankets of the water just like us. At the pool's bottom where moonlight cannot touch them, moonlight emoting no warmth, they might dream and when they dream, we are certain it is of paradise.

pink-grey strip of irregular
focally smooth with areas of ragged, pink
The deep cul-de-sac revealed a flame lesion
focally cauterized pink-tan
surface of the tube is pink tan and smooth
cm tan-red piece of irregular
consists of two tan-white, smooth, cystic structures
a small focus of orange tissue on the outer surface
to reveal tan-yellow, smooth, gelatinous
was quite globular
The outer surface displays a tan-yellow soft material
and blue-black lesions
The cervical resection site is inked black
The serosa is pink
filled with clear serous fluid and brown

Anything I wanted to taste tasted like paradise to me. The garden teeming with everything I sought to eat and I ate everything I sought. I consumed and consumed. I fed them, all three of them, despite the sickness they made it our paradise.

Beyond the high bare walls that hide paradise, more nothing, the dry, the expanse of sand sweeping over the dune grass. The wall is a trap meant to deceive you, meant to conjure in your mind that which was never there. The body absorbing the twins back into itself, so the specialist says it will. She knows her horticulture. And then the paradise of the body inside you, still greening, maybe a garden after all.

When
the walls of the
garden started to burn and
the garden had grown over, the trees
shuttered their branches, curled their leaves
in and slid back through their trunks into the
earth. There, they laid their pollen. They fed each
other each other. The acorns red in the soil, a black
crown of hair emerging from the underground
flood. The body inside out, scorched and ruddy.
Roses and their thorns everywhere.

Werewolf at the window.
Wolves in the snow in the woods
behind your house. Their paradise is yours
too. Darling fear. Darling desire. Darling flesh
red in my mouth, sweet sting on my teeth. Let's
rip this body apart together and lay waste to the
glistening between our legs. We can always find more
to devour. Paradise starving herself, coming on and
off the different drugs. Paradise shrugging it off and
hunting with the bony pack. Paradise crawling
into the white tree wells in the woods behind
your house. In paradise, they say you
just feel like you're falling asleep.

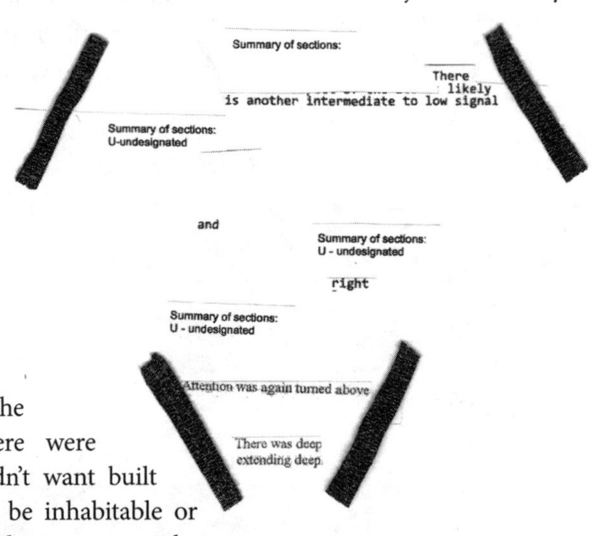

In the
garden there were
no houses. I didn't want built
anything that might be inhabitable or
that a ghost might wander into one night to
haunt. I didn't want any chambers, pantries, or
beds made up for sleeping. When the nurse asked
how many miscarriages, I said oh, two. Just two. And
she studied me like I might not have said the whole
truth. In my mind, the twins together were one. Maybe
it was three? Does it matter? I'm sorry she said, but
I have to ask. It's fine I said. Am I fine? There's no
obvious house here to examine. To wander the
halls, to knock its walls. Garden void of
tender structures. Garden just the
way I like it.

When asked to leave paradise, I was already
gone. I broke all the rules and gave zero fucks.
Really there was just one rule, but one can feel like
many in paradise! Especially in paradise. So utopic
we just want to burn it down, feed our desire for
destruction. Fire is spectacular. Leaving is better.
Is leaving better?

There are no funerals in paradise. Especially no funerals for bodies calcified within you, for them there's only scraping stone like mud from the bottom of your shoes, blood crusted on your face after smacking it on the door frame. There are no funerals for what's long been dead, for what was dead the minute you knew about it. There's only a bag for its medical waste. No cemeteries in this garden, no earth shaking loose from its stones, making way for little graves.

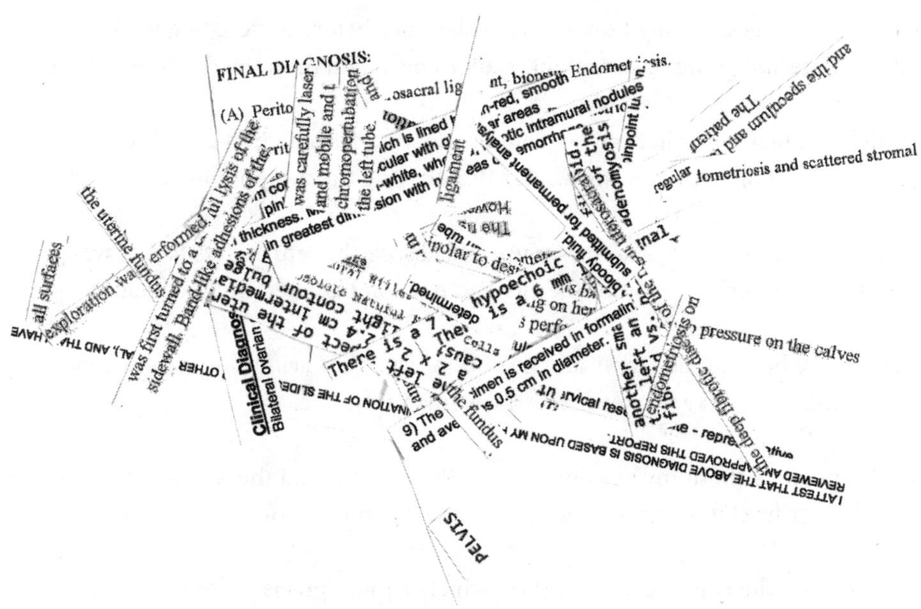

If the dead can't have paradise. Where will you go?

Where will you go, if the dead can't leave paradise?

To everywhere that isn't paradise inside myself
To water, to hanging, to rock
To push all the water lilies under
Spikes of their petals against my palm protesting
To everywhere that is
Paradise beyond me

Ode to Darnel (Ode to the Crocus)

To the early morning charge nurse Darnel who escorted me into the operating theater
where in my cornflower blue gown and goose-pimpled skin beneath a bleach-slubbed cotton

robe I was laid pugnaciously sobbing under the ignited, rotund surgical beams that blared
nearly through to my core where they would cut into and discover—I swear, the air laden

with the way the scalpel approaches flashing—you are the bright stamen of a crocus
on the late March morning on a Sunday while I walk my sister-in-law's dog with her

and discuss our marriages, a thing I did not consider once before undergoing the knife
except that the knife and going under might result in my death or in the discovery that I

might later die, and I have no alternative—said the doctor; he thought it could be quite true,
and after a week of trying to process his words, disbelieving them even, I finally

was able to ricochet "cancer" against my spouse and absorb the return if its flail. It was just
a few hours before we were to leave for the city and our son had mercifully, conclusively

fallen asleep and we held hands limply and he said *we don't fuck with cancer* and I conceded
his point. They could just take whatever was the woman from me.

But I insist this poem is about my love for crocus (and Darnel) and the way the flower insists
upon spring the way he clutched my reluctant arm, as if come hell or high water I

would break through the rime ice, the word for which is more precise in less empirical
languages. The no matter the weather, rushing the earth into and out of a season—

it's the no-matter-whatness about the flower that I've always loved (and that I felt in his
embrace) and if you ask me what my favorite flower is I might say a blue rose

because of the love I have for the first thing my spouse ever gave to me and what it means
so many years later, the petals unworldly and ethereal and spellbindingly impossible,

but I've never seen one rise in the wild as does the crocus that makes my cheeks flush
with its ivory velvet in delicate contrast with the blackened slush kicked across it,

the cardamom stamen brilliant against our strict winter sun, how it carries the deep glow
of daylight within its cup unfurling to clutch the sun's imperceptible emissions and guide

them into the depths of its root, and the impossibility of its presence each spring the
impossibility of chlorophyll when I encounter the brilliant blossoms fully flowered

in their stocky clump. Crocus, you are tender and blooming like the sickened ovary
the oncologist plucked and bagged from my abdomen while I dreamed I was still sobbing

on the matchstick-thin steel table, while the other was freed from the sticky web of adhesions
spun by endometriosis's relentless, gangly nest that's ruled my body since its first

menstruation. You are the uterus clipped from its stem, leaving behind the network of root,
what led to—

flowering in the vase or sliced lengthwise and flash frozen, your section beneath
the microscope of a pathologist scanned for wilt and waste, a cluster of majesty brimming

from the ground, and I tell whoever I am with even if it's just myself of my love for crocuses
and then days after: crocuses and days and days and days and then the year after

in anticipation, their arrival and the scans and then another spring and another.
The luscious purple not even anything like that of my insides, as if I could know, but saintly

and smooth and crisp and purposeful. Silk on my fingertips. The sturdiness of them.
The charm. Darnel, how I loved you for simply squeezing my hand I will never forget it,

for how you nearly carried my drugged body down the corridor which seemed
like the longest and the shortest walk. The impossibility of the crocus. The impossibility

of cancer. The impossibility of kindness. The arrival sudden and clear like danger
and also maybe something like conditionless love.

Swans! Swans! Swans! (The Sick, the Lovestarved)

I couldn't help but stare when from behind the bullseye glass above the embracing 12th
century canal and within its algal-lined moat waters I spotted two swans rollicking in Bruges,

pressing the flats of their foreheads together, the result of which was their forging, was the
ridiculously overromantic shape of a heart. Nor could I help but photograph as they floated

impossibly steady on the velvety gunmetal surface, the heart's interior peak a black snip of
beak made by the agreement of cinched cheeks, by webbed feet conducting each bar beneath

to steady themselves—cob and pen, pinned together
                                        the way later in Rome when toward
                                    the galleries, wherein the life-size women
                                    are cast in stone, suspended in poses

of imminent or current assault, I, too, couldn't stop myself, adrift and flapping through each
filigreed room, their subsequent chambers and one-way traffic of fellow tourists stifling,

snapping pic after pic in the congestion, fraught by arms blocking off the openings of doors,
and with no exit therein my breath caught as if gagged, a mouth glutted with dry cloth,

gaping at the swan gaping at Leda's faultlessly chiseled nipple. The swan's wolfish grinning,
his webbed feet raptorial, more talon than open-palm clapper snapping eagerly over his

knees, beak near puncturing her draped thigh, and Bernini, whose Rape of Prosperina also
therein is displayed, could be considered an exuberant centerpiece even—Pluto's fingertips

clenching the alabaster marble of Prosperina's polished haunch as he hoists her, praised for
how lifelike—clearly had one thing on his mind, or perhaps it was the commissioning

Cardinal, or it's we who gather, who pay admission to stare still, to remark at how exact the
acts appear, admire the violence against women slapped into the comfortable muteness of

stone set at the very heart of the yellow wallpaper gallery wherein too many desires already
arrive upon us at once—a need to edit down our lists of individual hungers, a need to be

parsed and sorted, to see how strange the sudden stranger is within us, the unchecked urge
we feel to overpower—timeworn and lurking, a hunger that grew on the mouth and

hardened into fact, not as much like the stone of Leda's body adzed back from its single-
source block, hauled by ropes cinched tightly across the bodice, by knots corsaging the cold

bulk of her illiac, the method of chiseling employed not like the painter blasting with his
expansive strokes the canvas, nor how his smear dries gradually upon the virgin belly, but

more an infinity twist, a repetition of the familiar—a practiced, predacious motion.
And to Leda: by some angles the swan looks to be trying to beguile from her her kiss,

as if any administration of reciprocity were valid. We are shown it is valid. His mouth near
upon hers regardless of answer. Posing what questions are unceasingly rhetorical. His neck

contorting, impossibly torqued, even more impossibly limber. But my god what strikes me
in all of this is how Bernini has Leda looking so relaxed against all that hard wanting.

The sheet slipping from her leg. As if to hold completely still in chaos is to be an act most
desirable. Is to be the embodiment of grace, delicacy, the solidification of poise.

How even did she manage?
So practiced. I remember in 1999, the resident swan of
Pottawattomie Park, like Zeus, also surprised us in his violence—the
lake he inhabited suddenly a single bird's stronghold

wherein he'd chase down any boater who dared cross its waters. His buttery body firing like
buckshot, bill hissing. And of course, my guy friends took that as their cue, took their boat

to the put-in, of course, to further provoke him, or maybe they wanted to feel themselves
fleeing, the terror of the swan's snarl on the backs of their necks, having never felt anything

like that at all. To say they killed him in their game. How easy it was for them to return
laughing as if wholly unchanged. Ask Leda, and she might say, there's nothing like a swan

at your starchstiff collarbone to make you go limp, to congeal, though I imagine, she'd
instead abide her reticent gaze, having learned the power of stillness through the excessive

practice of stillness, through praise. For shouldn't we have known swans can be *so cruel*?
That anyone can be, really? We are warned and that's what we get regardless of want,

of whether it's more painless to make the swan our villain or to leave him behind locked in
the darkening gallery, the disquieted lake, to turn our backs to his stone mouth, to the almost

of his barking-back mouth, the way it came upon mine, for instance, when I was only hoping
to sleep on its couch. The park swan sick and "lovestarved" had his reasons, as did Zeus,

imagining himself scorned when adorning his body in the silly costume of the swan, his idea
of what a woman would most want, not knowing the wants of women at all, his ignorance

catching him off-guard—that is to say bewildered, making him desperate, or ridiculous if
we're feeling generous (and to the men mustn't we always to be safe be generous?) As for

the swans in Bruges, who knows what comes after that honeymoon. And the statues? When
I finally freed myself of the gallery, I fled to the Garden of Bitter Oranges, back against the

dripping espaliers, my breath heaving over the violet skin of a sea of iris. No more marble,
babe, so finished with what men can make, with our dumb admiring how they sure can carve

up a face, and with mourning and mourning and mourning my waste and waste and waste.

Robin Returning (The Surgeon's Vow)

At some point, we have to make peace with the body's spent sweat, with what's tried as hard
as it claims its tried its best. My body, for instance, at a standstill, refusing to heal any more

than it has, the disappointment in quitters with which I'm familiar, making peace with the
peace clearly already having been made with or without my consent. And remembering how

the surgeon told me I'd be cured of my endometriosis really comes back to fuck with me.
His promise cloying like those of so many pretty boys, hot in my ear at the party when our

chests press together in the dank basement corner of the frat, floor awash with smashed
bottle glass, or in this case, while my undressed legs dangled off the sterile steel table

covered in brittle exam crepe, leading me on. And to believe in the possibility of reason
is also not unlike when that fucking robin arrives at the side yard after his many months

away, god knows where he's been. At first, I'm back too, deeply in love with his bright
orange breast, so well-fed and puffy, so dapper and flouncy. Then days later I'm hanging

last year's photo of a 4-color hawk face at the window whereupon he won't stop ramming
his reflection. I'm not so territorial. I'm not so *hard fact.* Am I? I'm not so wedded

to the idea of a thing or even to a thing itself, except for maybe hope, which is not at all
the same as reason, which is how the surgeon caught me, flashing the possibility of its

reflection teasing. And before he said *cured*, I hadn't even considered the probability. And
after, it was all I could think about, my crush, falling for that protracted monosyllabic

language. But understand! Since teen-aged I only wanted to be what one could easily erase,
doubled over in the locker room shower after each track race, overdosing on pain meds,

gagging in the bathroom across from calculus. In all that covert fight, I could never control
the organ's blight, nor the way it made me disquieted. I lived too long without second

guessing that, waiting for the appearance of a reason for what wouldn't have one yet. With
hope in soon disappearing. And we know how that ends, just ask the boys who only

recognize me in the dark. I don't think the surgeon discerned birth- from hallmark. If he did
maybe he wouldn't have sworn a little surgery could coronate a goddamn matriarch.

Though, like any confidence man, my guess is he would have all the same. So eager to
remodel me. And maybe that's enough to forgive myself for imagining, knowing how little

we can expect from each other, or perhaps that what's reasonable is only receiving more of
the same, except for how much I'd hung on his easy words. Could I forgive myself, him for

that, for how I came to trust in spring the way he described it? He'd peel all the lesions away
from the surface of every smattered organ, dig them out from the ligaments, the muscles, the

dirt? He wanted me to be impressed by his proposal and wanting to be impressed, I was,
envisioning the time my uncle took the entire skin of a mandarin off in one piece with his

ragged winter thumb, the citrus not sweet but cinder, or when my high school boyfriend tied
a maraschino cherry stem into a knot with just his tongue. So charmed I was by the

possibility of executable charm, of the grass greening all around the robin's ridiculously reedy
legs as he skips nearer to the subterranean window against which he bashes his head.

Dear lord. How can we animals be so stupid? We're conned by such low tricks. Unable,
even, to see ourselves in the glass beholding back, our reflections warning don't fucking fuck

with that. And months after surgery I was puddled in the darkwater bath, my thighs on fire,
and the flowers that newly bloomed inside me still wanted their wrath, stems thick already

with rot, petals brittle at the ends, the opening sticking back onto its familiar self. What then?
They were the kind of flowers that make your house smell like a dirty mouth when you

return home from a long night out, breaking down in the vase within which you tried
your best to pose their pouts. I could barely breath, nor apprehend. The pain so blinding, so

unlike anything that had been. How? And the surgeon's vow too, so brazen, so *we can still be*
friends, so *I promise it'll never happen again.* I'll be so good you'll never go back to the printer for

more hawks to tape against your glass, you'll never have to twist down your blinds at night
to be rid of me, leering just beneath. Who am I kidding. It's me tricking me, listening

not the same at all as hearing. Every word sugarsugary, insisting any of this resembles reason
when I'm as wrecked as the deranged robin, as unwilling to negotiate the terrors of mind to

body. We're both willing to perish for our convictions—it's not we attacking ourselves but
our reflections. There exists only exterior threat of action. And this time, we won't be fooled.

The Gulls (Hearts Were Flitting)

When the water is windswept and turbid, the breakers less like delicate keys thrumming
hypnotically, the elegant purr of a piano scale when fingers ripple cleanly down the

instrument's backbone, and more like hard slaps against the packed sand, when the lake is
the same carp nose gray from the shore to the skyline, the same goose pimpled surface

undulating imperfectly, more unpredictable than anything, the hungry gulls falteringly float,
bodies caught up in the gusts above the tips of the cottonwood holding up the dune, wings

stretched over the hard air currents, over the sand through which as much is visible to them
as in the water, wherein yesterday I watched them dive as gracefully as gulls could dive into

the surface and pluck herring after herring that, having given up, hung slackly at the surface,
stupefied, and their pearly tails flashed half-heartedly from the gull's dull beaks as they

dashed over the tops of them and into the air, wherein they would swallow their catch and
repeat that same greedy gesture all morning, they feasted, and even near the shore gathering

one, two, three, and suddenly six. It's true, I've never considered gulls as birds that gravitate
toward each other like geese, like cardinals, like starling, vulgar as they are, how could

proximity, how could tenderness come naturally? And it's true I've never seen seagulls even
touch each other, though I have seen them collaborate to signal and distract, I've heard them

shriek and conspire, their ugly rasping harks, shearing the space between towels lined along
the burnt-sand beach as they celebrated having emptied the contents of a swimmer's purse,

the Cheeto-lined pockets of an ex-boyfriend's jeans. And this morning, too, after I told my
son I saw an eagle soar past the window, his expression was unfazed on the FaceTime

screen. I said he didn't seem hungry or cold or in a hurry, just passing, the way a bald eagle
might, the way a sated predator might, under the cover of nothing, bored with the same

hunting, the same scurrying beneath him, the way a man on his way to work will keep
walking the same crowded path each morning singing to himself the same irritating tune.

That's how you know you're in America, my son said, and we laughed. Of course, he knows
already there's more power in our talons than our tongues (the trick, of course, to learn to

use the tongue). The gulls, the plover, the hummingbird, too, respond accordingly, retreating
to the interior of the ashy cottonwood. Even the jay ducking in the dune grass. And after my

son and I said goodbye, I thought about how what I might have said was that we also know
we're in America by how our feelings of sanctuary change from state to state, city to city,

forest to garden, by testing the imaginary lines scrawled, the borders between the base of the
lake and the air full of gulls and how overnight all the lake's clear depth for hunting is only

turbid water ready to pull your body under, and I wanted to say more about how danger
hangs ready inside us, a gull waiting to pierce the surface with its thirsting, an eagle flexing

hard along the beachline, daring anything to try him. Certainly, the national bird wouldn't
ever appreciate the fear and relief one could feel on a cross country road trip, knowing at the

border there's some sudden law against him, or not, or the shocking relief a woman, having
been stripped of her uterus, having already had her necessary abortions, the selective

reduction, her impenetrable euphemism, might feel when her feet hedge four corners at
once, her unmedicated procedure involving such careful impalement, a thick sterile needle

through the skin of the abdomen not once but twice, to reach the uterus, to reduce three
budding bodies to one, the success of which is predicated upon passivity, not flinching at the

very sight of the instrument, the pressure of its steel in the stomach, but instead melting into
the surroundings, gray sky in a gray lake, becoming more bed than occupant, more dune

than bird nesting in its grasses, and how unbearable, how much more like betrayal, denying
the instinct to fight back—though at least, finally, here we've arrived at the heart of the poem

about an eagle and gulls, neither of which I ever loved much anyway. And now I love even
less, though I'm working on it. I'm in recovery. The esurient birds' bluntness stripped of any

majesty, especially the gull, a straight scavenger, loner, user, tag-a-long, plundering garbage mouth. And there are so many names I, too, have conjured for myself, which change like the depth of visibility of water depending on the day, depending on whether I can look at anything hard enough to see it. Sometimes the voice of the doctor saying *you'll die, you'll all die*, ringing in my ear in the morning, her voice the same voice that said I didn't have to watch as my spouse told me the story of an island where the waves made no sound upon the shore, where the sand was just as bright as the love I had for our one maybechild, the one I hoped to save, and for myself who I also was trying to save, I think, I think I was trying to save her. I don't know what I saved her from. Sometimes the voice in my head mumbles out the words I spoke when I saw their tiny figures curled into each other, sharing the same micro-placenta, on the screen before I can silence it with the clasp of my hand, when I saw the needle entering their bodies where I knew the doctor knew where the gathering of cells that would be their hearts were flitting. Sometimes it's the voice in my head that reminds me I said nothing after all. I could only watch what was happening to me happen to me, a stunned fish on its back, belly up at the surface of the water, head dipping toward the depths, the pressure of gull beak making me suddenly dizzy. There was a chance we could all die, wasn't there? But wasn't there a chance we could all live? Much smaller, though, right? She said that. There was a choice I had to make and I made it. And sometimes I think the voice in my head tells me I didn't make it. That everyone else made the choice, and I floated instead like a gull over the surface of its water, searching for the lone fish separated from the school, for any glittering evidence to feast upon, anything certain to chew and swallow, to feed the eventual wreckage in my body, something physical, something obvious, something I could dive into and maybe never resurface from. I still feel that way sometimes. Sometimes the gull. Sometimes the memory of fish. Sometimes the licked-clean bones at the bottom of the frozenover lake. Sometimes the gull in the sightline of an eagle who would know, just by the height of his soaring, all the business below him. No one is eating today, so stop your

trying. He knew my secrets before I knew them myself, borders dissolved at such a great height, wanting me to take the risks anyway, choke down the shimmering lie before he could

swoop in and kill me, before I could martyr myself on more turbulent water, if that's what I really wanted. If there's still time.

The Binaries

Eclipse

Easiest to calculate the mass of each body based upon the way in which one passes over or in front of the other. We're not saying either party is correct just remarking on what is. As in how the pair learns to finish each other's anecdotes. As in diplomacy. As in the one's stories are now the other's. Belongings unpacked fair game. As in the elliptical route must occur on the same plane as our line-of-sight for the perfection of the effect to be fully appreciated. As in parlor tricks. As in jests made from firm footing. As in my shadow is equal to or of lesser value than its eclipse of yours. As in there's an observable collapse in brightness, a sometimes disappearance of the lesser star, especially when the dominant one becomes so feverishly piqued.

The Tulips (The Cervix)

Before I even saw their perfect heads, the violent reds piercing, the petals together screwed
tightly in the dawn light as the sun tried to rouse us from our beds for another day of work,

before I could even change from my pajamas, my sleep bra, throw my wildly tangled hair
in a tie and walk outside, they'd all been disappeared by the deer, having caught

sight of their bright spotlights, beckoning them to slip their pearl-ringed muzzles beneath
the silk dress of night as they strutted the sidewalk, stumbling over each other

and into my front yard. No one was driving by and not even the dog barked when they crept
nearer to the window, bent their snouts beneath the thorns of the rose bush and ravaged

the ruddy blooms. I wonder what they tasted like or even if the deer desire them the way I
desired them, longing just to see them radiant and bobbing in the spring, made a little manic

by the pollen dust that swathed everything in its radioactive yellow. And too, I wanted to
kneel beside them and wonder into their cores, my whole face where only the fat

bumblebees had once rested, drunk on nectar, drunk on the taste of fleshy tulips in
springtime. I wanted what I wanted but what the deer got to first. Like on the operating

table, after slicing into my abdomen, after the frozen sections came back negative, the
surgeon reluctantly followed my orders, taking only what had to be taken, in order to spare

me my cervix. We'd reviewed a list of options together the night before, having a sort of
three-way with his girlfriend who was booking a cruise for them, we were all on speaker, she

inquiring about the half-day jet ski tour, I telling him that I wasn't willing to give up my
orgasms if I didn't have to, and when we were finished giving our reasons, he said the same

thing to both of us at the same time: *whatever you want, just book it.* I was so impressed by his
multi-tasking (I listened patiently as he read out his credit card number, expiration date, cvv

code), and even by how he treated our desires more like ambitions than inevitabilities, like
the way I feel about the tulips once I spy them beginning to swell, knowing I'll never see

their flushed double ruby cups unfurl, the deer so much like destiny returning to my
doorstep, the way they are always hungry to devour things down, to take what they want and

make no apology. But a girl can dream! And after the surgeon followed our best-case
scenario and left me with as much as he could leave me with given the tangled field of

wildflowers he'd found inside, having pulled everything rotten right through the midriff hole
we decided we'd make, he used glue to seal my stomach back together, to force the threads

of my muscles into recoupling. I think they're still working it out. The scar fading. The
wound beneath still tender. I might always be tender. And it lets me know it's there—my

decision, my desire, which sometimes feels silly and selfish and meaningless, especially when
after a long morning run having pushed myself a little too hard, the severed muscles clench

like they're wringing out the rag of me, twisting me into the ground, down next to the empty
tulip stems erupted, their two dejected leaves flopped against the black mulch on either side,

their soft juicy green smooth and striated, where I say out loud to them that I chose this, as
if they care, and also that I chose to sleep through the cold spring night when the deer came

to my door and smashed their faces greedily into all the terracotta pots, their hooves clicking
on the concrete, tongues licking the insides of the cans collecting rain, the way the cervix

might receive forgiveness for its crime of wanting to remain, for trying to rouse me in the
night to watch the rangale in the act, or to save the tulips the way I saved the measure of me

I knew I'd always want later, if there was a later. I'd always want later, wouldn't I? Even if
later is only next spring or just the next after next. Like the tulips—perennial. For however

long it was, I'd want that.

G. Amamiana (The Medical Waste)

I've never met the Japanese orchid that refuses to bloom—its mousy, stomach-like bud
lurking wild and nubbed in the leaf litter, in the black understory of evergreens, canopy of

chinkapin oak—never scrambled through thick rain into the thicker temperate rainforest,
moist beneath my slicker, to spot one along the underbelly of a trunk turned, felled by the

hoarse roars of winter, over where already what's died is covered in a shameless, fevered
moss which I guess we must admit takes over everything eventually (thinking of how rabid

the earth is in all those apocalyptic zombie movies), turns the ancient trees back into their
forest floor, giving them ultimately what they came here for, the old ground below calloused

and suffocating, a buffet of regret and swarthy orchids appearing barely beautiful, tubular
above the fungal humus upon which they feed, looking less living than living dead, never

blooming nor it their intent, I mean, just like my uterus(!), prohibiting any organic element
a haven or glimpse of its knotty, furtive viscera (until, of course the steady hand comes

willing to cut itself in), and for the orchid the effort with which to expose itself would be
enough to instantaneously kill it in the same event, equivalent to the death of the ugly organ

snatched from the dark forest of my abdomen, its splashed blood having fed on my tissues
like the orchid on fungal nutrients, power hungry and vampire-esque. And since the surgeon

snipped it free, my phantom sex rudely accosts me with hybrid plagues—pain interminable,
desires permutable, body dreamsniffled, waterlogged and whirled like rain in a black gale,

a tawny sickness of such aching for what's apparent but unseen, to want back what
unapologetically extracted my autonomy from everything, the missing a persistent tang I

can't clear from the back of my throat, the lesions the trapped blood left blaring, my self-
made toxicity, and considering, too, how all at once I became sexes free, floating, wild and

rangy, like the lowly orchid leaving the butterflies and bees out of its own replication entirely,
my understory stripped clean, having endured the fitful narcoreverie: my sister and I pressed

palms together under blushing green leaves made lightless by a husky mycological night
rising whereunder the lesions performed their final acts of siphoning, and she asked,

would I have otherwise been? Still XX or XY?

So cracked wide, a subdued vessel for an oncology resident's first incide, the organs'
concealed call of leech and surgeon's answer to ardently debride—having been folded, stuck,

bent into submission after more than one try, my throat raspy from where the tube was
pried, my ears ablaze with the question of sex and seed, which is to face the question of

the amamiana orchid that keeps itself shuttered indefinitely, refusing entirely the act of
photosynthesis, its fungoid grifting, bearing fruit despite having flowers that will never open.

Could I have lived that way and never opened? Will I refuse to bloom now or thrive without
organ? What offering can be made from parts of the body flash frozen, sectioned

tissues, lobbed like refuse into a wobbly silver basin, tumorous and unchosen, the nubs left
sewn and constricted, everything sick burnt beyond recognition, my loss as invisible to

anyone's eye as the orchids who remain deep in the shadows of oak hide, hermits in the
swampy woods found (remarkably) alive, burrowed in what was knocked coolly down while

we all so heavily anesthetized. Was a proper uterus ever there? We call it barnacle. We call it
fried. We call it dysfunctional relationship. We call it big lie. And the orchid? Resupinate,

folded and glued, similarly fit to be tied. There's no ceremony for our shuttered organs,
Flower, no formal bidding goodbye, no ritual in the forest where women gather to dress

such sick and abandoned brides, kiss our scars, show how to take up our ruined parts and
reconstruct our lives. No. There's no burial for such foul growth, such withered things, no

divinations demystified, no drooling animal to later dig up them for eating, just a mass end-
of-the-day medical waste burning, a hospital's pseudocide, no eye to have memorized, to

even look twice at the little bruised ovary and its crushed velvet ties, the uterus's reliefs, carbuncles protuberant, black and blackening (what maybe tried its best if we feel any

miniscule hint of generosity), to conjure any sense of finality, to grieve, later maybe, if we even grieve, at all anymore, a little bit, by any means.

The June Run (Menagerie)

On the first evening—which was one of the last of June—that I caught glimpse of a firefly
dizzily alighting at the corner of the neighbor's patio, three in fact, and what they were

deliberating, I couldn't say for certain, not knowing fluently the language of firefly, though
perhaps they too were relieved the plodding rain had already blown through by midmorning,

that the haze of its remnant against the heavy peridot blades of grass was a slow vapor rising
hot around them dipping drunk on its slog, blipping, low-slung at the ground, or perhaps

they were wondering, like me, whether the wildfire smoke would in fact descend tomorrow
before dawn, burning the backs of our throats, planting its harsh scent of raging

conflagration all over our manicured yards, forcing us to remain closer to our made-up
beds than we'd ever want—the aphids were also furiously assembling in cumulous clusters

along the edge of the lukewarm lake wherein, as well, forty-two mute swans preened and
dunked their burnt orange bills into the loamy pool up to their necks, bobbing buttery tails

skyward, up through the gunmetal water, and someone in our town's online group asked,
why am I seeing forty swans in the lake? Which made me consider whether I, too, wanted to

know, or whether I preferred to linger in my curiosity, its space like the one made by the
hard flat surface of a table and the body seated in its chair, the hollow knowledge makes for

us between our desire to know and our actual knowing, one a delight, the other a disaster,
always, interchangeable, the split wherein you're not one or the other but what moves

interpolated, delighted by your own refusal to sit or stand, to eat or be eaten, to accept that
something must be one way or the other, like having to call a coyote a coyote, an aphid an

aphid, a swan a swan, or even a swan a sparrow—your own refusal to recognize what inside
yourself is already all of them muddled, and too, a menagerie, already the fox, come home to

itself in the blackberry den wherein the table is set with itself and itself is sitting in its place at
the head, arms fixed on either tufted armrest, sweaty fur settling into the creaking frame,

expectedly. Where are we right now, exactly? On a run by the lake, in between the space of
question and answer, in the body in between the body and the table, floating within the bevy

of swans? No, of course it's only a bevy when the swans' feet are flat on the squishy ground
not paddling languidly along the surface of the water, all eighty-four of them required, the

act of which defeats the purpose of such gatherings, as the point of such amassing is to
create the illusion of impenetrability, to outnumber what would come to kill at least one of

the white birds, but what hunts and kills a swan I've never seen in action, what might upend
their bodies—the same way they dip below the flat surface of the water to gather pondweeds

and eelgrass in their mouths, to fill their bellies—but just with more blood, alight in the maw
of what predator devours them, the sparking metal and flint scratching against feathers

against teeth. Don't you know there's no setting a table for that? You can only dim the
chandelier if it has a dimmer switch (did you install one?) and if not, you've already done it

all wrong, fucked all the eating ambiance, good job, no swan for you, no place setting, no
chair with your scribbled name in front of it, no knife under the crystals sparking against the

ceiling like slow firefly scintillation rising up in the night, having overslept in the hard ground
and been slow to learn how exactly to ignite, to speak in sign, what the flashing draws down,

damp, out, and what it means to be a newborn body made of burnt-back embers, drifting
over the sidewalk to the neighbors', nearer the swans, nearing the aphids who, too, are

restless and globular like the pale green eggs laid in the lake's marshes into bulrush nests by
swans, their lawless swarms not far from the same buzzing inside of you when all the while

you go on and pretend it's otherwise (go on!), a wild animal having been unwilded in the
wild all around you on your last run in June, and deny it all you want when the wild comes

wanting you to sit at its table head, imploring at the very least you make polite
conversation, running toward you even when the night starts to fall down (and fireflies are

the only chaos map to home), its hand on your neck, its mouth on your back, wet and
unforgiving, your hand on your neck, your mouth on your back, little living—you'll invite it

in. You'll invite it to return, coyote, fox, swan. Firefly, sparrow, the aphid—a hundred stuck
against your chest, their cornicles, their honeydew, their slender stretched mouthparts that

would pierce the skin of everything set before them, exigent in its green rising, the riparian
garden where they suck back trim tart sap, pucker at its briny nectar, refuse to dab the

corners of their mouths, too, to wipe back their cheeks, their greedy faces, welcoming
instead more feral to settle upon them, to soak into and soften their exoskeletons

long after you arrive home, breathless and limp and, too, quite as famished.

The Daffodils (so high I have to step off)

I told the daffodils I wasn't going to come back out until they were gone.
I said it as if they would care, as if they weren't busy unfurling their awnings in the 7am light,
as if they all bloomed at once and died the same day. How silly I can be.

But, am I as silly as a lovesick daffodil, bobbing my bright yellow mane
over the sun-licked pavement, swollen, sloppily drunken on my flimsy stem?
(Haha, no.) The yellow of a daffodil so much like warning . . .

or it's the color of friendship, or it's the color of whatever I wanted
when I ran past so many of them, planted by the eager volunteers,
their efforts supported by a city grant,

the daffodils rising in numbers each year and still the bulbs arrive by the truckload.
What can we do but sow more until we're overrun by their obnoxious beaming?
And what does a daffodil smell like? I don't dare

go any closer, nor should I want to find out, the way I should keep my distance
from you too, whisky on your tongue, careful not to consider each pulsating tepal
appearing above the unedged spears of natant grass,

the bleary red mulch, the wet mahogany of the aquatic park, as
I run over its bowing planks set above the black mud, so many fucking daffodils
setting my mind in a twist where the scent here is all just

so much earth (and so much overtaking me now), I can't
pick up anything but the damp of last week's rain, the sweetness
of moss and bark, sweat surfacing on my hairline and beading down

the back of my neck. Maybe danger is more possibility than peril. A mouth begging to the ground
instead of caught testing its own weight by the prying wind—heads bumping into one another
recklessly, so why not add more daffodils into the crowd?

I could put on a dress the color of daffodils, but it wouldn't bring me any closer to you.
I could cut them from the wild and bring them to my dining table but there they'd only embolden
me to stare at them until they died, and what if they didn't die fast enough?

How long can a daffodil last, clipped from where it sprouts from the overripe ground?
I'm not sure I trust myself to know. What I'm saying is
I'm not sure if I brought them in, I wouldn't end up somehow falling in love. And I need

to keep my distance, to keep the reasons to deny the possibility of tenderness nearer
the way I keep my breathing level on my run, not harried, not fluttering by how overeager
the coronas are to light my way, lovebomb me, throw me off guard, raising my heartrate

so high I have to step off into the neighbor's yard
and hold one hand on my chest, count down the hard wild beats, throw my arms up
over my head in surrender, close my eyes to all of them. They're blinding me. They're

all I can see.
Fucking daffodils.
Fucking daffodils.

Annual Scans (The Procrastination Run)

As someone who currently longs to know so little,
I can't tell you everything we lose,

and I have a feeling I haven't yet really lost much
at all. For instance, I still wear the bright neon yellow running sneakers

in case anyone comes looking for me in the woods,
curled up in the beds of deer, napping in the thick of their warm bellies,

damp in a dream of me sleeping between the clement dreams of deer.
I have a feeling I don't really know how bad things can get,

not yet anyway. And too, I have a habit of feeling lucky
to have escaped what I have so far, like the cancer

that took my friend away so quickly. First she was better.
Then she was dead.

And still, knowing how sudden, how steep
the precipice is within the commonplace dream of falling,

I can't book my scans, can't FaceTime the radiologist.
I let the oncology nurse's calls straight to voicemail,

preferring the mute company of the rye nests of deer.
Or, oh I'll be on my run by now, treading

one of the same five trails, waving to
the crossing guard as a way of waving him the fuck off.

I don't want to talk, unless it's you. I don't want to see anyone unless . . .

I block Sloan Kettering's calls and everyone else's.
I let the run wear me down and over

until I'm too quivery to turn even a door handle.
I pant rudely, sprinting into the congested park, scattering gravel,

my pulse raging and nearly faint.   Let the world go dark.
Now, please.

I have to find the phone number for the imaging center.
Just Google it already.

Just leave the country.
Or transmute into a deer. Do not disturb.

Or, I'm here if I'm needed.
But don't need me, okay?

Don't summon me
to your radiant unknown,

to your screens black and white
to snap your million photos,

field of tricks, pursed lips, to press
the hard wand against the organs,

to sempiternal scans glowing against the brash lightbox
when the specialist phones,

opens her mouth to say
whatever she's going to say.

The Binaries

Contact

The closer the bodies drifted toward one another, the closer they came to actual touch, the closer they encroached while passing a drink between them, the first stress test of back and forth. Of fathomable generosity. As in the fulcrum is never the same as the center of mass, and it's best to keep that detail readily available in order to account for how one body is always nearer in proximity to the eventual pivot. Also known as inevitability. Also known as aggressorship. Also known as the point of no return. How close is the question we're guessing at. The guessing far longer than the gesture itself. As in at first it was a thumb grazing the inside of a thumb, surveying the gravity of elasticity further. As in the palm stayed steady as a firm means of quiet reciprocation. From there was determined a tangible durability. As in the elements released on crash contact were mostly metals, were heavy glitter in the solar winds, scattered recklessly, sparkling; impressing the grounds of the bodies of both stars.

Azaleas in the Vase (Whose Glittery Wings Falter)

Like the azaleas under the endless daybreak mists, keeping their mad honey locked
in their stamens, their shrill fuchsia corollas, all my expressions flowered and burned at

once. Utterly feckless, rashly my heart perched on my sleeve, as it's not been known to do.
How, then, could I have caught myself before giving into you, into my inside self

moreover, my absolute appetite for nectar too palpable, too pressing, too letting my guard
down against my guard who stood panic-stricken, frozen by the shock of seeing me go

against us, like ohmygodwhatareyoudoing!? Then perhaps a little thrilled to feel such
deviation—such changing of the guard when the guard (me) grows tired of my same steely

attire, of the way the musket stiffens against my shoulder when the deep chill of the moon
suddenly recedes from its former dark side, the dark side I came to believe was the only side,

having lived that way a little too long, like the hummingbird whose glittery wings falter after
having gorged on hastily arranged devotion, now sickened by its overripe, its persistent

nectar leaden in the belly, too glutted even for flying, for hovering, for darting away from
skulking predators, I drank whiskey like water and hit the concrete spinning. It served me

right. Still, the warning was one I preferred to interpret as a gift, as in I made choices that
brought a black vase teeming with azaleas to my doorsteps—they are beautiful and they are a

threat. What did it say about me to welcome them so, that danger, to water it, place it as a
centerpiece inside my quieted house and stand dumbstruck, suck at its intoxicating presence,

unapologetic desire, gobs and gobs of azaleas, their quick and certain poison and yet, the air
between us—its molecules frenzied, dizzying—just what I was looking for when I hadn't

come looking at all. And what if what's hanging on the end of my tongue is what brings me
later to plant more azaleas in the weakened spot in the side yard, where the earth is full of

white mold, stringy fibers like the gray hairs of the hoary willow in winter, where I insist that
something thrive when obviously the soil has long since corrupted—azalea over and over.

Surely familiarity with lack is enough, isn't it? Surely wanting a thing so badly makes it
materialize—this belief a kind of reckless persistence, while the more I planted them, the

more they kept dying—azaleas incoercible, nor could I force the ground beneath to change form,
the flowers refusing to bloom in the wild of the equinoctial nights when the deer tiptoed around

them, knowing better to leave their hallucinogenic flowers to the lesser creatures of better
proximity, to the truly starved of us, who'd wander out our doors at night to fill our hands

with them, with the dirt beneath them even, going madder by the minute, the way the
hummingbird is just spinning above the shrubs (what is she doing up?), and knowing that

now, thinking about how such brittle vows rolled easily enough off our tongues, were
ground down after a hard day gouging out the rot so heavy and dry in the mouth, venom of

longing glowing hot on our lips, splinters in our fingertips, in our throats dense, bitter when
I try my best to breathe someone else's reasons in, (that's a lot) when I say what I want to

the ones I want (also a lot), I'm certain it's not the fault of the azaleas of course, which can
do nothing but bloom their stupid blooms, their clusters of radiant flowers indifferent,

helpless to do anything but blind the fuck out of you under the afternoon sun, but light the
way to where I never exactly intended to go, to where the mud is soft in my hands when I

fall into it, to where cold fingers pinch my soiled dress, showing mercy (mercy a thing I once
mistook for devotion, aglow as mine was), to where I leave my waiting at the door, clothes

plucked from my body as if they were nothing more than a weed contrary to the abundant—
fragrant and brilliant with young azaleas—garden, their sweet and spicy, their clove, the

azaleas who'd already long let the peaceable birds drink from their cups the intoxicating
nectar of their drenched coves, but not without consequence—not without pressing hotter

pleas to the surface, syrupweights, demise, the danger viscous on our chins, the almost of it spilling out, and the way I easily could let myself refuse swallowing flower after flower all

over again and again, each one from each vase sweetly annihilating, but won't.

The Alewife (Jerry)

It was the summer the alewife ran aground early and the summer before they closed
the beaches at dusk. It was the summer after the child nearly drowned in the quiet waters

beyond the first sandbar, and it was the summer I lost my favorite necklace to the hungry
sand in the dark, whipping someone's abandoned charcoal grill into the sniveling waves that

breached clamorously against the shore, stepping over themselves nearly, their vulgar
complaints keeping coming, warning us to keep our feet out of their spray. And it was so

many summers ago when he was still alive, Comstock, or Jerry, but really Comstock because
that was the street he lived on the end of, or maybe it was in the middle, and we called each

other by either a last name or street name or the name of the bicycles we rode until alone
together in the muggy tar of midsummer behind the undressed dunes we'd settle on a

blanket above the snake grass below the vapor passing under the silvery stars that seemed
more like holes punched into an expressionless sky, shrill pencils snapping into thirsty paper,

and we were looking through each other that way too when revealing our real names, at last,
like the sunken vessels we thought they were, knowing after we said them, we'd be past

return, we'd never do it for the first time again. And, too, over the mounds of sand, it was
the summer the bonfire on the beach was overeager and raging where our friends were

urging each other to hurdle over its flames, which only grew stiffer when one kept spraying
lighter fluid onto them, the flares ripping up the line of liquid and nearly exploding the bottle

in his drunken hands, and the alewife, my god, they must have been so sick of themselves,
too, by then, as they began to flop their bodies up onto the sand, up onto where they would

no longer be called to consider their mistakes, their gills instead huffing against the tiny
tawny particles, saucer eyes wild the way they are when caught in the act of swallowing a

disguise, the shimmering bismuth sinker and the hook to which it's tied, their guts already
spilling larval crustaceans from their contents into the hollows of their fish bodies, the way

surprise mixes with desire and gets everywhere suddenly. All evening, all into the night they
flicked their smooth figures up, the sound sharp at first when the broad triangles of their

heads exited the water and then the soft flopping slowly gentling them into place on the
shoreline, the dull black spots on their shoulders going still when the waves rushed up over

them, up to our beds. We didn't stay together, and it's not because we knew each other's
names, nor because of the way stars like us are intent on devouring every planet in their

sightline, nor for the alewife who came to understand that what they'd invaded was
landlocked, a body of water they could never be free from, having lost the canal they could

never stumble their way back into, the one-way ingress to whatever was beyond the black
night ocean water around them, the shad lures shimmering in the distance, and so they lived

to kill themselves upon the beach, to turn the shore silver, quivering under the hooded light
of the moon and against the fire which wasn't illegal then, like so much else. When

Comstock was alive. When his skin was already yellowing, smiling a toothy smile, in his hand
a bottle of Popov, or was it Crown Royal or Beefeater gin, the memory of his body already

far drowned, the sandbars long behind him, or was it the summer before all that, the
summer before he died which was summer after summer after summer after lying in the

dune grass, feeling it spark against my legs that hung off the end of the impractical crochet
blanket, its tickle proof of what holds the land together, keeping each miraculous dune in its

undulous form, from sliding out into the water, from finding its way along the bottom to
that other universe deeper in the earth than any lake, even ones that hold the surreptitious

positions of vanished cargo ships, deeper than any knowledge of their names, than any lair
an alewife could swim to, and so they beach themselves, they wreck themselves, they

disclose themselves, locked in as they are, locked into their dying in a distant place, in a place
they never meant to endure, a place they wished beneath the stars would just fall down on

them, the summer before that and before that. It was the summer of having had enough. The summer the alewife perished in spectacular fashion for miles along the shore, their scaly

bronze heads a scintillating sheet that smothered the gold coast. It set our mouths on fire. I can't lie. We couldn't even bury them, as many as there were, and Jerry, too, gone before his

liver could finish him, wading into the same endless body, neck deep in the reflection of the driest, the hungriest stars.

Old Dogs (Clip to Your Neck)

penned dogs bay at high fences
lunge to the ends of leashes
whimper when I run by dreaming

hyacinths, emerald ivy tights
sheer on beech trunks, riverbank
brimming and ruddied by unrepentant rain

give these dogs a little water, some clarity please
there, there   sweet boys
no one's getting off chain   no one

means any harm   means
we'll control   means what we want we reign
double wrap white-knuckled fists

bright collars lift on the necks
voice boxes clipped, barks hoarse—
I don't mind it

don't mind any dog anymore
there's a lead for each
even you and you and you

leash of synthetic braid
leash of lattice, gold inlay
leash in my prim hand

double fold I clip to your neck
pat you on your head
old dog   baby dog

tow you toward me
leash clenched in your soft jaw
offering (good boy)

loop nudging my wrist
leash on your canine tip
tugging—want to rip from my grip

the summer dogs especially sweat it
white spit, tongues drawn in
or hang off slack wet chins

soft chain shimmy spin   tousled neck
I'll clip my lead to that sweet
wreck darling dog I'll pull you down

The Quartet (The Shore, the Peony, the Palm-reader, the Sugar)

1.

I can't say for certain what fortune I might have walked away from when instead of home I came back for the smooth immutable edge of glassy water, its crystal spilling over the shore's daybreak-honeyed lip where the very peak of the sand, too, was glistening, where the water's body soaked through every blonde grain itself, each glossed remnant, each sun-bleached arm of driftwood, each pocket shovel discarded by the children playing near the very edge of its percussive waves that spread their palms across the waist of the beach, scaling fingers along the shoreline's backbone, utterly devouring it, and the water was like the sky itself, alight and silvery, its skin too just beginning to warm to the suggestive touch of the sun—which was still emerging from behind the peak of the dunes' silky bluff—upon its delicate shoulder. What could I have imagined that I hadn't already buried myself beneath? Having grown tired of living with just the bite of cold sand between my palms, its mucky grains rough on my tongue, grit raw in my teeth, of the view from my underworld being nothing more than nightfall, more wet and musk in my nose, here in the beach under the squeaky sand with all the bones of birds and fish that washed up last year, the same falling asleep to eager plovers running up and down opposite the waves above, that when the shivering wind came down hard to the south, it seemed like as good a time as any to tack just as hard. Its fingers purling up the roots of my hair and sparking their flint on the back of my neck with cold splendor, waking me anew, my feet replied by coming up too close, hasty even, to the water, aching for more tender gestures, for my legs to be swarmed by its breakers where the curling shock bit into the very tips of my hip bones and filled the arches in my sneakers that were already long caught in the sand—I decided for once I wouldn't turn away from my own wants no matter how cold it might make me, even if it meant letting the messy swash rush up and over, knock me back into the ground. No doubt I'm still shivering. My time here is borrowed like so much else, and no doubt home is trying to cut a signal, but before I go disappearing back into the earth, dissolving into a gathering of pin holes bubbling at the hard shore's surface, I want for once to join in the chorus of the greedy who care only for more, never tiring, never an *if* about more (they say *fuck no* to asking). I want to be the endlessness of the possibility of water quaking against the unrepenting coast which is also how fate found . . .

2.

me on my knees in the garden delicately drawing out the dead blades and last year's decimated stems from the shimmering crown of a single, sudden peony. I was good, resisted every temptation to move too fast, to risk interrupting how the renewal buds were feeding upon its bashfully petrified legs all winter. And wasn't I lucky, as you once said, because a peony might only bloom every other year, and here the richest blossom was ripening on the end of its stem over which my stunned jaw was stuck agape at the pink bulb upon a stalk already as high as my hips. I took everything that had done its best to flourish the year before, that had spent a season beneath the snow, turning rough, turning liquid, turning like a wave into itself and melting back into the earth, all to feed this bright new pomp, its lip leaves glossed with a sugary sweet sap that could draw every ant for miles to lap up whatever they could while the flower, awash, unveils itself so achingly slow. We're happy considering the ant's delight until the peony becomes laden by its bloom and the visitors upon it, fainting from its own weight, from the sustained effort it takes to be so desired, face falling in the dirt, the very reason I sneak behind the weeping cherry tree to lift its little altar, its fragrance refusing to stay where it falls on the tongue when I press the lusty velvet petals against my cheeks, knowing if I peeled back every feather from the bloom, plucked them each away deliberately to try to find you beneath one, even if the bomb were thousands of petals, I'd still come up wanting. Fingers sticky with sap, palms covered in a swarm of ants horrified by what I've done. But this isn't about saying I'm sorry. This isn't where I say I'm sorry. I know...

3.

I've tried sitting perfectly still, which is harder than it looks, maybe you saw me? As in you can see but you can't have, and everyone has to learn how to be fine with that, fine with holding your hands in your lap, fine with the peony's spice and citrus on your breath but not in your belly, fine with dirt under your fingernails and in the lines of your palms your childhood friend once tried to read while holding an apple and a palm-reading book, one in each hand, she said your lifeline was forked and windswept, she said your love line was faint, a loose yarn of wildflowers, what the distracted children lazily strung together, the unfinished ends of all the stems branching off and messy, not to be stretched lest they unravel, sticky with the sap of flower sticks snarled, and maybe you'd never know how to love at all, and that the lines of money, sun, and head were all crossing over one another impossible to parse without wrecking the skin, like the way the waves smack the beach and smother each other when the tide changes direction and the undertow is stronger than you at first grasped, sucking heavy at your ankles, ripping back the layers of reticent sand and churning it, changing all the rocks into stones, changing all the stones into what you might later skip over flat water when it returns, counting aloud as the surfaces slap like palms against its glimmering skin, dipping but never breaking, water much tougher than you thought, the concentric circles rippling away into the nothing they were before you got there, the stones treading out into the horizon, further than you can see afield before finally being pulled under, did you imagine it? Was this in that fortune she gave you? Try to think. What did she read to you while she devoured that pink-fleshed apple? Its juice glazing the back of her hand, running down to her elbow? The words at the end of her mouth. What were they? You should have listened. Should you have? Listened when she said you should just dismiss the idea of loving, run on home, be more the way the peony unfurls, its perfect, tantalizing pink—temporal. maybe ~~it could be~~, maybe it is more than enough for you, and you just want to know what exactly is enough for you...

4.

How can we even take our eyes off them? How can we refuse getting into the garden with anything we know for certain wants us there too, slinking as close as we possibly can, heads low to the ground, to whatever desires our tending to it, tending to its tenderness, tending to the tenderness we find within ourselves when we're all palms in the musky dirt? We are more tender there, aren't we? Vulnerable as we are to our own physicality—like the peonies and their own weak necks, their own way of arriving, every year the possibility of more blossoms on the same frail stem if you let them feed on themselves, if you give them so very little—how can we not love them for that, the way we love the lustrous glass of the lake's endless shoreline, running north until where we can't ever see the end of it, spilling all its contents at once from its brimming mouth, offering it all to us, we who have no way at all with words, are well unearthed and awash, the water so unable to help itself against the force of legs, the hem of a skirt as it is? How can we not want to watch every particle of water disappear back into the earth or cup them in our hands and ask them to forgive us for not loving them better, if that's what they wanted, or maybe for loving them better than anything else in this world when maybe they hated us for that, or the way we might love a peony, the way the peony would never love us and that's what's most needed here, something more like desire not destiny, a thing we can offer our whole bright selves to, selves without fortune whose mouths feast on the dead to be ripe with the living, mouths at the edge of the water somehow withering, somehow, still, there's thirst, an indelicate chorus at the edge of them smacking the sugary gore of apples, licking down every grubby contour of every open palm?

Sweet Pea (The Mendelian Paradox)

It's July in Michigan, so of course I'm utterly preoccupied staring off into the persuasive pink
seas of sweet pea, the exact origin of which is uncertain—like us, as spontaneous too perhaps,

so we inform each other more than once, that we like it that way, and to perform formal
analysis would only yield incomplete results at this point so why bother, and, too, even

Mendel's painstaking experiments with the pea plants have since undergone such extensive
scrutiny it makes it that much easier to cast the practice of gathering data aside, to remove

science from the equations before us, knowing further study can only lead to further
inconclusion and our subsequent inability to accept there's not much that desires to be

definitively answered, that the translation of all of this is the elevated potential for Mendel's
research to have yielded results that were too good, too highly sought after even, to be true,

meaning, plainly, that the greater the longing, the greater the improbability of the math
to demonstrate the tangibility of its ceasing, and the Mendelian Paradox therefore

permeating, as well, my own field of vision wherein my particular senses are not to be
trusted (don't let them say otherwise!) deluded as I've become in the presence of strange

wildflowers, which is to say in the presence of you, where all these blush meters stretch for
miles—wherein, nearly dreaming, I, nearly swerve into the deep green ditch wherefrom the

florets rise—nearly—nearly ridiculous in all this course overcorrection, in my falling in love in
the dark with at least a thousand flowers at once, and do you even care just a little? Me

telling you all of this out of nowhere. If not, oh my god how embarrassing, or if so, go ahead
and stay, be as reckless as I, wander, too, into the field into the unlit and billowing rye

surrounded by the humid petals of the sweet pea, the depth of the trees' nightshadows,
which seem now like they could swallow and put us to sleep. And we should already be

in our identified beds when instead we lounge in these deep floral nests, which, too, are
dizzy over us, thirstmad, their flashing magenta, their endlessness, their relentlessness, their

readiness, their dazzling pink so deliberate, so unapologetic the way they spread their
voluptuous beaming across every grass hedge, every woodland, do we love that yet? Can we

love that at all(?)—what's entirely for our pleasure—the sweet pea—even if just a little, allow a
slender bliss, what we've since forgotten, made ourselves forget, how what hangs its

intensely gorgeous face in front of ours before persistent absence can only drive us as mad
(as it did Mendel)—undone by elusiveness, can only stab, can only hedge the math, but then

how heady the scent that draws me in regardless, thorny when I do my best to be kind to it,
not to turn my head from its leggy stems, under which I'm whimpering, the velvet green of

their foliage shivering, the sweet pea's gorgeous winged gash, unabashed blooms doubled
into one another not unlike the bleeding heart, nor the petals of the labia, not unlike the way

our mouths react when inches apart, the mania, eyelashes quivering against such recklessness
(or for such recklessness?), the possibilities of whatever it is we can't take back, and there's

so much I might, lying flat in the grass, tempted, thinking of it (or would I?) What difference
would it make? My face pressing all the same into the hearts of the flowers I gathered in my

hands along the way back to the same bed that greets me regardless—creatures gathering
where we gather—and I think about how the sweet pea first came upon me, or was it I it,

both of us warm (it's July after all), soft even, I might say if I remember what it is for
something to be soft, to be pardoning, to recognize the touch of what has no intention of

harming me nor I it, that there could yet be some science to this, to what only wishes to
hand over what's been wanted—the sweet pea—darling, persistent in its benevolence when

we're alone with ourselves, when we can't even give ourselves that which we've been given
(no such depth to our kindness), when in our dreams we must both ask and answer, wake in

the nest of honeysuckle heavy air, yet the flowers' indeterminable origin, saying yes, go
ahead trust this. Does that exist: the data I desire matching the data I collected? Or, maybe I just

forgo all these silly ideas about science and paradoxes, submit to what distractions I can plainly see, this temporal pink-pink sea, the near nownownow nearer, nearly of you lying

back down with
me.

The Binaries

Heartbeat

Stop me if you've heard this one already. It starts with a poet and a star and a heart. A two-, no, three-body problem. The poet taps her finger on the bar, less hoping to draw attention than a service. Whatever comes next is surely every consequence. The star flutters its lashes when the tall drink of water appears, never having tasted nor seen such sudden sweetness teeming. The heart hangs its head, just wants its whiskey: its bottle and a glass, if it must take a glass at all. The writers all roll their eyes. The teens come to play their dance beat music over the speakers, liquids pulsing atop the counter. The star sees something it maybe remembers in this concentric movement, the proximity of shoulders, the skin upon which is soon as slick as the fingerbeat heart—the no-good fist tied safely up in its relucent coronal pericardium. Still, they enjoy watching what enjoys itself. As in red and yellow together appear orange from far away. Nonetheless we're mistaken to see them as such. All stars a choral something. An 808. A mulish thumping. The writers just groan. Whatever it is, they say, it's still more stars and hearts! It's more contemplation of gravity than we're up for right now. The poet as a provisional barycenter knocks down the drinks with her elbow as she talks. Proof of existent force. She is clumsy but trying to be tender. When the glasses fall, they shatter and the liquid is everywhere spreading, a signal the heart knows is time to go home, but the star keeps confused by. They are gentle allies. At least, they were at first. The poet was generous to bring them together, even if it was (a little) by force, and when she excuses herself, pushes their chairs closer to cover her absence, the writers will claim they saw it coming all along: the gushing cloud of ardent metals. So immediate. As would any star, or heart for that matter, commence the immaculate genesis of its binary.

Lay your Obsessions (A Feast for Wandering Stars)

Cake Breaker

The invitation stands until it doesn't, until it, like a worn-out thing, inelegant, tattered, hangs limply from pinched fingers, dangles above the rest of what's been deemed useless, until the star, continually dissatisfied with what's on offer reposes itself, impolite as it is in such circumstances to request seconds, pushes back its chair from the dinner party as it were—too much low frequency conversation in these backlit galleries, text speak raking its way across delicate sponge, all that gelatinous slow spinning. Not enough hard metal, nor present metal *metal* enough, and there's been sufficient helpings of candlelight flutter to last its tramp to the skulking backrooms, up the lowlit staircase—bright lips pressed against the silken flint of forks, of amble of overworked preamble dribbled—certainly, for one evening. Don't you think? Are you following or no?

Toddy Ladle

Out in the *vaster wilds* of the interstellar marshes, to the places where doomed planets align themselves to be devoured down by starving stars is where we can better get acquainted, if I'm honest, where we can dip ourselves behind the bar, sink into our own neat drinks, where to partake in such acts of desire is much more like acquiescing to hunger, to rejecting what comes to be sated, where what is unable yet to act against its nature has its way of returning to us for more. And behind the bar's locked door, stars often find themselves running low on fuel, nearing empty and wondering how can they answer for having exhausted themselves this way (and to whom do they answer?), having sweated out their quantum talcs so recklessly. There's nothing closer to nothing to say here which is the only state we've found can invite in a little truth. Knowing this the stars might finally let loose their hair from its bonds, might let at least a taste spread on their tongues.

Lobster Pick

And if we find we're too much alike, if the eaten heart eats the heart that's eaten more than its fill, sliced its hand on boiled shell, we can still call that an accident even, chastise desire for its willful feasting, prepare a table of quiet forgiveness between us. After all, I don't want your sorries, your storied excuses, but more your sorrows. I want the darker part of your heart, its deepest shadow, to settle down within mine—to be something insoluble I can work with. Hungry black hole that eats and eats and stores in its cooling chamber, in its lightless vault your every whirring, confession confessed for future replay, for later consumption, that I am.

Salt Cellar

There's a gathering of particles, a smattering of whiteness moving through your body, everywhere that might be a place we can imagine this happens, thousands at once at every millisecond so the theory theorizes. And some white holes are a one of one, catching like hooks at flesh—a sliver in your heart, having rubbed too hard against what's left unfinished, make a begging in the middle of the night that stirs you sweating. But baby don't panic; I'll not be petty like you expect, a particle keeping you guessing at my brand of pain in the dark, whether I plan to stay or go, not having arrived to fester anything like the small talk we hate. I'll instead make a lithe light behind that thumping thing. A warmth I know you'll like. I'll show you how it is between stars, how we're above all that scratch and burn, that blister for the sake of blister.

Sardine Server

How long can we persist—back and forth, the brackish energy of each binary impressing its silver scales upon us? One day I won't know who to show up as and neither will you. We'll see whether we like that. I only think far into the future for this very reason. I want to avoid any conflict of orbit. Our instincts far different than our appetites and only so flawless. Because really, how do you work up the nerve to serve the same oily dish like this, offer the same taste to the discerning tongue which only grows more adamantly fastidious as it's fed? The same salivation no longer wet enough for every mouth that's outgrown it. I want to make us new, be planet-swallowing stars. I can't be sorry for what I've done, not even just a little. I want a parade of pretty worlds approaching, to take my pick from everything eager. Not more mushy bones and dead eyes. If set to music, you'll see I won't complain, not even a little. I swear it; there's only hunger here.

Caviar Spoon

Of course the genesis of all names was first a sensitivity on the very edge of a tongue awaiting what eager mouth might speak it, the desire to name a form of grace and recollection imperative especially for those of us without the assistance of photographic memory. How can we know a thing at all until we're able to articulate its methods, its materials? Until then a nebulousness, a persistent almost-forming in the stellar dust that may or may not settle, depending on which direction the solar winds carry our particles, deeper into or out of the insuppressible interstellar grasses, into them waist high, into their greening all around us where we take each other to seed in what's hidden, buck and bray the names we claim for ourselves into existence, the hungriest stars having ruptured. In our mouths how we never expected them heavy, and what's the name for that? The name a name we cannot conjure having seen only its rough onset. The subject and researcher of the theory will, of course, die with their findings before any conclusions might be published.

Strawberry Fork

Our appetites are wider than our openings wherein whatever lodges appears just as black, the opacity of which would terrify even the best of us. And weren't we terrified at one point or more? In this, we're lucky we're the best of us, or at least that we like to think so. We wish others the same providence knowing how easy it is to fail altogether. And when. And that, yet, we might as well. Here's to trying! To knowing how it's only when you step into the dust of the diminishing star (and if you breach the orbit's threshold you won't know it was the threshold until you do) can you see what it is made of. Its sweet. Its seed. Its eloquent billowing. When, immediately then, you are, too, the very same. Welcomed. Awaited. Wandering star, you are hungry as ever.

The Weeds (Accidentally on Purpose)

I watched the first weeds burgeon and decided this was the summer I wouldn't stop them,
every inch of crabgrass, every foot higher the woody stem of nightshade, the rogue lily of

the valley bells that slyly migrate, and the hardwood scraggle of spruce, a bluegreen that
somehow found seed in our hospital-cornered flowerbed. God I was so tired of all that

order, of the clattering of stacking trays, of all that black mulch spread between the lilies for
which the deer came in the dead of night to devour anyway. Who was I keeping things so

prim for—just, after all, myself, and maybe the neighbor's sense of me which was also for
myself—the work of caretaking, nurse-maiding every rock-lined border somewhat satisfying

until a week of lavish rain, of tangled-sheet dreams, the same slogging offer of harvested
reprobate grass was presented on my plate. No appetite. Would rather go hungry than reheat

such arduous leftovers. The irises and milkweed soaring regardless, even as the neighbor's
forsythia twined its way into all of their aspirational bedrock beneath the visible face of the

earth, its secret sickness, its slick nightsweat. *So what,* I countered, some things are doing just
fine coordinating with their ruin. What's the worst that happens—after all weren't the

neighbors even more uncaring toward their landscape, refusing to prune back the tree whose
branches made moss on our gable shingles, the same tree whose trunk is full of paper wasps,

of carpenter bees? And further afield stronger substantiation: the town taking to mow the
yards of vacant houses? I mean fuck it. When faced with all that overgrowth, doesn't some

large part of you want to watch it manifest more, just a little bit, to see how wild things really
can get, how close to wreck we can let ourselves step without gripping the back of each

other's shirts and ripping the body back from the very edge, if we can see it, see how deep
the weeds might sow their roots before we can no longer resist choking their arrogant necks

and pulling them up into us? Knot at our bellies. All that hair cuffed in your fist from the
seedling grass now grown in, a little nest of immaturity between the stones, all that vinyl root

ripping up the surface of the ground, threatening to take the gentle stems of the morning
glories with it when it goes. Maybe we should let it? If it's true there's no longer room for

weakness in this world, and isn't that how we've come to see fragility? There's no scheduled
operation, nor overbooked surgeon, nothing to cut neatly away from what's already been

taken, what already has taken over, nothing to shape or mulch down just a commingling of
fluids in this wild bed where everything comes to exist synchronically, roots wrapping roots

regardless of origin, of belonging to, wringing the water of themselves out bit by bit. A
healthy sacrifice under the right circumstances. And if I want that, if I'd hoped for

something less reactive and more Darwinian, something to happen from a safe enough
distance, a low-stakes opening where I refuse to intervene, to rewild my own urges in the

confines of our rust-fenced yard where the tiger swallowtails return to the hairy green
perches of the rough leaves of purple coneflower that lie open and arched against the

afternoon light, resting wings pressed together upon their lance-shaped faces, there's
opportunity, if I can get myself to see it that way, to accept what I can make by refusing to

act, or rather by acting out the very point of refusal, holding my arms at my side, while the
grackles plod in the yard pulling up blowfly larvae and carpenter bees, how maybe they

might love me indirectly for such inaction, how that could be the good in this, seeing how
they begin to arrive in flock and stay long like the swallowtail, plucking over the electric

sheet of grass in need of a good cut (nope!), how they hop into the wild of the weedy garden
and wet their silver legs on its dew, probe what's buried in the cores of the hostas, whose

shady cups maybe they drink from though most likely not, it's too romantic and they're not
here for romance, nor are we, its time-consuming preparations, but more some form of beauty

we already well recognize, the flashing heart which comes only by unproven exercise.
Probably, too, for the feel of the air upon their wings once they emerge from my snarled

labyrinthian green on green, to slowly catch chill when airborne they flee, goose-pimpled, awakened as any grackle could be, as any one of us could be, that way, if we so wanted, belly

full, if we let ourselves free.

Glories of the Snow (get on your knees for it)

The snow glories with their fat mouths gaping only shrugged when I warned their jaws
would overfill with rain, that even too much of a good thing like water can lead to ruin.

There's a draw I feel to this type of insistence. The sensibility that surfaces in times of
drought and some of us, it's been found, are better flowers than we thought we could be

in times of record need. I know I wanted to trust the flurries' glory bed even as their
outrageous apertures remained gasping for water, even after they'd all had their fill and

stayed starving for more. I figured they must have known something I didn't, spoken a
language beneath the black and green earth that kept them satisfied with their hungry, their

knowing that April only lasts so long, and that soon their violently blue beds irradiating the
yard would disappear overnight as if they never were, as if I'd never seen them wet and

luminously naked blushing constellations shadowed by black clouds against the blacker
atmosphere, as if beneath the grass duvet, between the silver-tongued stones disintegrating,

they weren't really tangled together, imbrued by the soil, legs awestruck in sheets, plotting
their next umbrage, but only stood next to one another, expressions stoic in the imaginary

squall. Anyone can put on a brave face for a day, a month, maybe a year, but who else can lie
underground waiting for as long, or resist the ground's freezing in the deep mess of winter?

Eventually all snow glories will appear, rising in the night, their bright ghost faces, their
furious chatter dotting the lawn, their sugary expressions glowing, lighting you down,

drawing you in. And there there's no scent then but the scent of you. I had it once and tried
to hold it steady in my mind. The scent of you wondering what glory of the snow smells like.

You have to get on your knees for it. Where the scent is your ear pressed against them,
bellies full of rain, and it's the scent of balsam fir when crushed, and too, it's the breathy

admission of wanting, the starved way the stems shudder, unable to keep up appearances,
iced mouths of roots drawing together. So low to the ground now, how can we hold back?

The Riot Fire (Attach Me Not)

I make you cum, you cannot leave, I drown my heart in kerosene
—2 Chainz and Lil Wayne, "Long Story Short"

I'm not sure if anyone here was bragging about playing with fire, but I'll jump in anyways
since I once saw it done spectacularly: the magic initiated by two teens after two fifths

of Jim Beam between them organizing the collection of car keys in a Tigers baseball cap, not
to ensure on-road sobriety, no, but rather in order to round up every Pontiac GTO, every

Ford Tempo—sparing of course the wax-glossed muscle cars, my friend's step-dad's silver-
winged DeLorean—park them parallel across the width of the street, pile upon them every

cigarette-burned couch after dropping each from second-story windows of the roughed-up
frat houses onto the solo cup dotted lawns, whereupon dozens of sweating sinewy arms pall-

beared them to the tops of their amassing burn piles. I've seen, too, the way sneakered feet
scramble deftly up the side of the peak, arms crossed with mixed kindling, term papers and

textbooks caught between clenched knees, and the way the boys crawled beneath the black
bellies of the vehicles, nicking the rims, were careful to twist the typing paper into cocked

cones, screw the dish towels soaked in Everclear into bottles or shove them into the tight
necks of gas tanks, blackout drunk as we all were already by then. Able to spare the liquor,

lucid as we felt, emboldened, the way worn down rumor was fisted into puckered orbs and
fed remorselessly to the greedy fire, the blue books, the latex powdered lab equipment, the

deflated footballs and the frat's lost and found empire of unwashed thongs, t-shirts and
boxers collected from beneath pool tables, the hi-tops without mates, ties unlaced useless

when separate, when employed to test their strength to fling Molotov cocktails at the inferno,
which, thoroughly alight, blocked access to at least a dozen apartment complexes including

mine, and too, your texts crackling up on the illuminated skin of my phone, stripped of all
identification—the only way of knowing for certain that it's you. And me? I'm fairly

comfortable around such disasters once they've started, the one inside your heart for instance
that keeps you melted to the roof of my mouth, a tack unbearable to scrape free, everything

tasting of your cloudy cinder, of what's flammable, already up and burning, and also, maybe,
I'm too easy, lingering over people effectuating their darkest urges, burning shit down

proclaiming things like, *preservation by fire, baby*. Okay. Whatever that means (but that was
your mom's car), a little bit of friction dolling itself up as untailored love, a thrifted number

appearing suddenly on the porch, aching to seem brand new, the difference between I don't
even care to know and knowing anymore. And what is that difference? Let's be clear, it's most

about the spectacle—on the scene count on me to be coming. I'll loom unfazed, covered
in the toxic antishadow of your blaze, the warmth of its wet smoke wooing me: doing my

best impression of keeping safe distance, never learning new names for instance, especially
when the fire raises a hand to my chest, meaning to block my way back home to where you've

drowned your heart in the caustic accelerant of me, drank it down too fast and vomiting
(I'm not sorry), from where all the kids blast their sound systems, Kid Rock and Trick Daddy

pouring into each other like hard gasoline pumped up from the tank underground, crop tops
stripped and belted into the fire which was so bloated by then. The moonface of it illuminated

every luring sanctum in every red-fleshed house, each window a mirror reflecting our edacity
onto ourselves, our refusals to yield, to put out our anarchy, which really was just whatever

comes before fire, which some say is smoke but we know better is desire, what we can't snuff
without tearing whatever holds it apart irreparably, not caring anything for how to incite a

spark properly, nor then how to tend it, careless as we've meant to be, to blow sweetly at a
kindling's neck to get it hot for us (use that tip sparingly it may only work the once). No this

certainly isn't in any way a love poem or a poem about fucking or maybe it is? I don't know.
What I do know is the way in which an ember can stick, can sickly sweettalk us into fusing

with it, how exactly we later can't explain what possessed us to keep feeding the flames—our
bewilderment lingering well after it was time to cut things off, smack the hands back, block

the texter of the texts, turn the porch lights down at least, christ, stop pouring on the gas—
nor how delighted we are at the same time to see a spark's genesis spiral out of control how

quickly, the fire licking everything pressed hard to its face—I mean, just surrender me. And
don't bother dangling relief—a vacuous persuasion—delivering its vessels too small for enough

water, stiff equations, offering to milk mud from the ground. You can't just mute what makes
even your hands wet thinking about it, where we stood as near as possible to the very edge

and saw the way in which the fire ate and ate and ate, so hungry for any one *thing* regardless of
what that thing was and saw ourselves in it, each other in it, the craving for more and after that

more, faces burning, positioned too close to the thrashing flares. We wanted that. And days
after, again, if I can be honest with myself even a little, remembering how I was immobilized

by the riot fire, its heat—stinging and relentless, its red lines rubbed into my wrists—was
satiating, that I not only saw but caused disaster to unfold, to refold and stuff the afterglow

into my pocket for later. We dug our heels in hard and it pleased, while the cops were called,
watching the fainthearts flee. The want to endure more than we'd wanted to endure startling

us. Hands on fire ripping up from the can of kerosene. You shrugged off the danger, the
probability of blowback. You attached. And when I, bluntly, love so very little, can't I at least

have love for that?

The Subliminal Message (The Surrender)

So you didn't dream it then, having not conjured what is helpless helplessly into existence the feeling
you hoped would bring a little relief, what hubris that was
which tucked nearer to your tender rib made a bunting, flicking
its white cloth in all directions, the signal of your deserted country addled on the wind, a
muffled squirming against the finial,

outstretched in order to restrain some softer self from falling out, that slight
construal you were maybe reaching for, too far outward as it were
leaving itself to the murmurs of the waves stunted by the glass of the seahouse, what barely
audible jealousy of what you couldn't bring yourself to say
but nevertheless

endured to be said, how it was so effortlessly able to disappear beneath the surface
having no memory of what margins came before, leaving you to study at the hard wanting for
warmth an unfastening of the gray skylights, the orange leaves dropping themselves
one at a time from the maple in a gentle teasing that also felt suspiciously bitter
before scuttling down the dune.

And the moon eclipsing the sun, the pair's ring of fire obscured by our hazy chariot of rain, its
particulate waterdust kicked up by the turbulent hurry of wheels and hooves,
was what you said you always saw coming, desire desperate and dirty in its approach,
still it's hard to let even the sun's smacked-shoulder burn go—after all,
didn't it make you feel, even if there was

willful pain, a little bit more alive? The stinging, these pressures of waves
rolling onto the beach so rough in their remitting, and crude
in their saying yes to whatever we think was worth them saying yes to
without thinking when we are
with ourselves stranded and looking for any kind of help,

which is also another interpretation of surrender, the water-worn wood
wholly exposed yesterday nearly buried now by the sand, its back long
dead to the touch, the surf smashing against it unforgiving, having held onto more
than its fair share of angers,
so much like the way

the body bit into the other as a means to draw blood, saying their togetherness
was a fated thing, just getting started then, the marks seen rushing for the shore,
my hand over your mouth like it was receiving a message to cup for later, the ache
pounding in my skull, every fingertip
having pressed its desired bruise.

Trying to translate the intimacies of it wouldn't help when to hear the language
of the waves makes us deaf to their little words at all,
they carry no apologies between their lines, between their legs, let's be clear with each other
when they want something
they are relentless

like the moon that pushes and pulls them and so far has not been so quick enough
in its leaving, and too they have their darker sides, they forget
about that easily like we, like the body that dives beneath their gelidity
their insistent surfacing—
resurfacing.

The Binaries

Vampire

From thereforth what else was there to consider, what else but the way in which each idea is suppressed by the force of the possessor star's consumption at its donor's very eager throat, having exhausted its own nuclear fuel, gorging on every speck of dust, her every scorching blue. She never knew such acts of hunger. Such cataclysmic variables. What near death can drive us to. Nor suspected such strong desire for the authority of them, their self-serving, fanged acts. Refreshing to know what's expected in a pairing instead of wondering what, precisely, must persistently be earned. The body relaxes into orbit and is to be handed over, every stellar component a belonging, an another's. So settled then. Two negatives tendered in choky embrace. As in when the distance between the earth and the moon is all that separates such terrible giants, it may as well be the space between two perfectly polished teeth and the skin of our necks, between sticky molecules in the blood—the enzymes, sugars, the antibodies, between particles of the soil pressed over the top of the possessor's face when it lies down for the day, post feeding frenzy, post cry and collapse of its dizzy donor star.

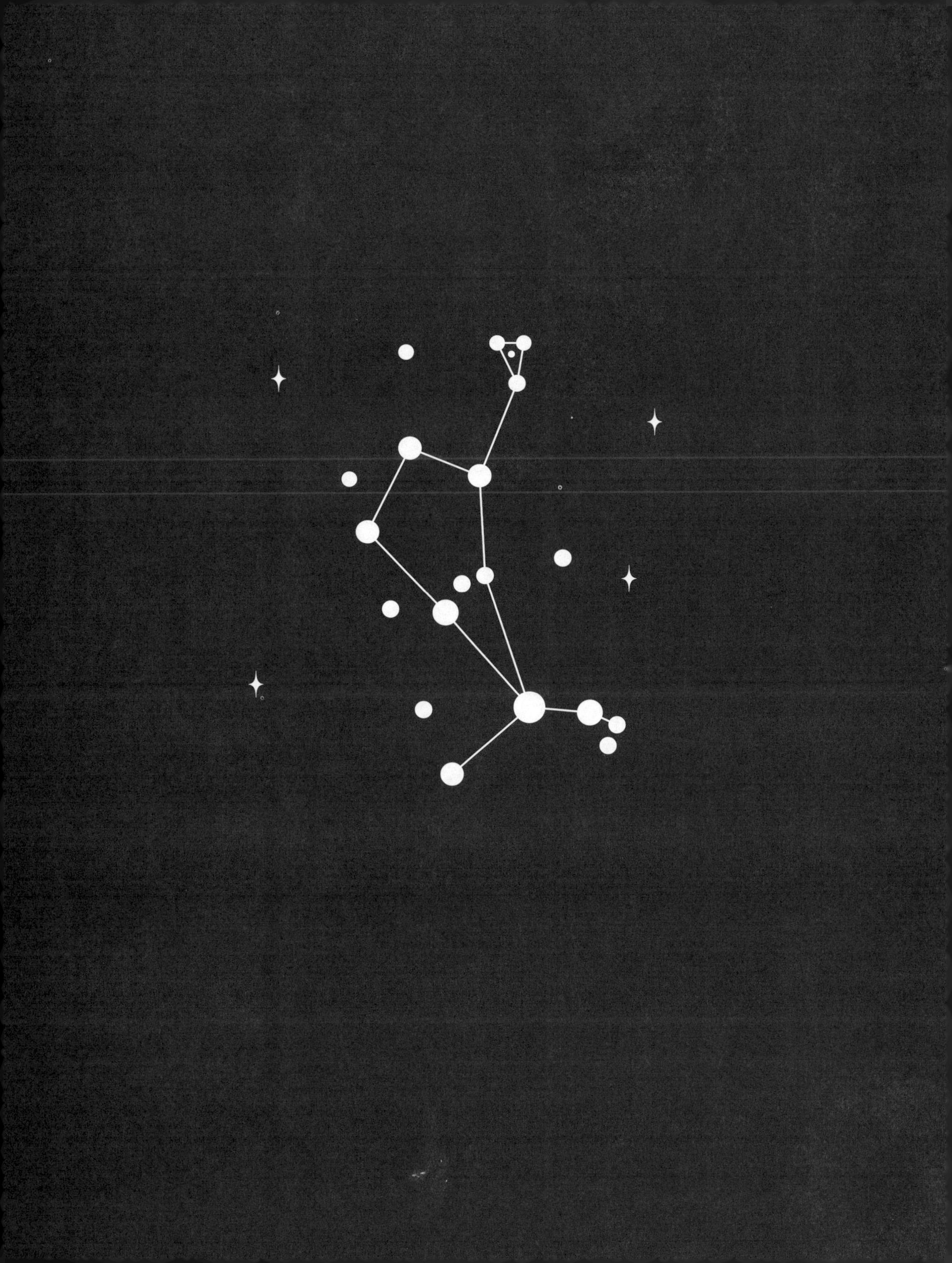

The Sirens (Undenied)

—ending with a line from Portishead's "Undenied"

When the sirens called otherworldly over the roughshod waters of the Tyrrhenian, Odysseus
had a plan in place, Capricorn rising he likely was, already knotted to the mast of his ship,

preferring to be dragged down with its wreckage than endure failure's putrid pomegranates,
married as he was to every mess he made, mess of insisting he hear the sirens impart

their interplanetary knowledge sweetly to him, mess he should have seen coming when
setting his men to grind their oars against their oarlocks—Ursa Major persisting to their left

and within her celestial bear body, the woolly stars Alcor and Mizar appearing as one, bound
gravitational to each other as they are—rather than risk washing up on the glistening beach,

risk a cosmos of sand in his parched mouth and whatever tickle of luminous silk came upon
his pruned feet—the treachery of what knows how to present itself to us as delicate (reader

beware), the binaries invisible to the naked stare, come to collect whatever survived thus far.
And like Odysseus I think it's best to keep a healthy distance between yourself and the stars,

intrinsic ability to wrench you into their orbits as they have, sweet with their mournful songs,
their Beth Gibbons contralto voice spilling from the cores of their massive bodies

that would have you quivering on the rocks of their hypnotic vibrato presently, where a
certain single star is all you can think of, its wine-dark incantation blistered on your brain,

your body incapable of moving in any other way than elliptical. And when the stars
warble, I'm sure they contest its only because of hunger, or maybe loneliness, definitely

for survival, knowing it's just always their need for more, for another you to have if they
can get that, such accumulation a dazzling proof of life, and, too, it's only because

the waves from their cores are percussing ceaselessly against their surfaces, maneaters
they've become, it's only their siren insides trembling out and over, them wearing their

hearts on their pulled-taut sleeves, trilling. And Jesus, you might really want to consider
something sleeveless to just avoid all that seductive crooning. Although it's said kneading

wax to press its soft pulp deeply into the wells of your ears can prevent temptation from a
chorus ever reaching you—if that's what you want. Just saying maybe try it—to reverse the

gravitational pull, resistant to being conquest as you assume you are, can't yet admit to being
the weaker star, the sirens hoping to turn you to swine or worse, the singers hoping to show

you through their smoky velvet doors, maybe to incinerate you, or at least fuse your metals
to their cores, parallax beneath their terse diaphragms. Forget the heart too high in its chest,

trying to force you to understand, consonant, in charge as it believed it was (laughable
really) as it once understood itself to be, a meteorite—impossible to stop once it got

going, restless inspiral, once it amasses, once it generates enough energy to power creation
on at least one planet, once it knows there's no getting away from it for you, from the brain

fog it pours from its mouth into yours, overserving its narcotic trip-hop, its ambrosial
battered vinyl melody, suddenly you don't know how much you've had too much to drink,

waves along the burning surface like an ocean in which you could sink (and come on, you
totally did). You could be deluded, Odysseus waterlogged enough to jump ship even if

you're not careful or refuse to tie yourself to the mast before the singing starts, if you start
tearing at the loose ropes, if all you want is to run off and dive toward madness, mad as

you are, but the stars know already what you do before you do it, waiting outside the bar
to ferry you home—dog with its tail tucked between its legs, dog who only wanted to

hear what will echo in eternity, ears pricked to retrieve every high pitch, every frequency—
even if it means destroying your own boat, even if it means stranding yourself upon a single

splinter of wood, shivering at the honeyed brine that washes aggressive in your mouth,
steering against the song that drives you steadily mad, while the sirens act so indifferent to

that (par for the course really). They could never get colder, so focused on steeling their own
nuclei, stars that they are, not on you as you at all, but on what makes them more forcible—

whatever your paltry musings only slow you down—ease the effort to draw you in with their
ghostly cantos—what you could never resist (silly baby) a good bewitching, what you

fall for every time, having been far from home for as long as you have, having considered
yourself above the laws (feel sorry for you, boo) of gravity, having been roaming the galaxy

looking for the same kind of star, having, too, already been the one amassing its own
orbitals, carrying the flooding haunt in tune ready on your tongue, never having set out to

ruin anyone but then look (oops) broken upon the shore, the hull shards of boats, the raw
bodies of the men who couldn't swim any other direction but toward your island, black

holes tugging at each other's belts shuddering, on the shore where dreaming is the sand and
your glossy legs upon it, dress whipping in the wind, (hi, lover!) trilling your hawktooth song

in their ears, its sound striking sweetly above strewn corpses in their field of bone and
flowers, field you lead them to, oxygen tight in their lungs, gravitational, generated by the

most massive of stars to keep them breathing—keep them alive enough to keep them steady
in orbit, come life or death, neither or both, either fate the same really, the orbit the point,

the promise of knowledge in all things eternal—Odysseus wanted the power of that more
than anything—which it turns out is nothing on its own, Alcor nonexistent without Mizar,

rider nonexistent without horse, is only feet erratic on celestial hum, its wavelength rocking
you recklessly, legs going limp at the ankles in the sea as the windless waves salt your eyes,

everything gone black, bruises on the fruit of your thighs, seeing stars at the pure heat of it,
palms suddenly heavy, the cruelty of lyric's beauty which, after all, ended up lacking its every

promised fullness, the last thing you hear before going under, envisioning the exquisiteness
of the mouth from which it stems, and still you can't quite see its source, which is ultimately

a relief, a relief to escape the torture of wanting anything at all when nothing at all you want
exists, to harness supermassive splendor instead of having to survive against it—reluctant.

Magnet. Siren, star,

release my whole desire.

Little Sparrow, Baby Mole (The MoMo Twins)

Don't come to me
little sparrow
baby mole
blunted blue
to the black morning road
anymore don't come
to me as the sour dream
seeking algal
velvet anchoring
seeking quell
the place I desired you
you dwell whirring
our shared burrow
all that throaty swell, the way
the organ mud
clears from the inmost well
what I buried.
Beyond any sallow
soil inhospitable
where I might rest
with you beyond
the quiet
chorion
where I instead deliver us
forcing this gruff purple sleep
our jellyleg
acquiescence a moving
apparition moving
right through me.
I watch it move through me.

We can't keep here
not one moment longer.
Catch chill
tip of my headheart
tip of my twintongue
notch where what umbilici
implanted come undone
they warn
I can't keep
you
catch chill ever-
long what I'd want stay
let root their entire colony
transfusing the garden of tarry fountain
ivy cord, rose vessels vermicular in
mobbed amnion
complications list unabbreviated
I can't even say how long
to get there from here
don't ask directions
discordance
sudden despair—
catch chill
if what the mole, what the sparrow
perhaps is nothing
came to be nothing
is just me
is just the dead
me
lost under my clumsy leap
and ever and ever.

I hope you will forgive my fluster
my crushing your forms
which are also my forms.
But if not, what can I do?
There's so much nothing
so much I hoped
to control over nothing
for nothing
with nothing as much
as empty in my hand.
To the many acts
of desire, to duplicity
a feeling I'm in love with
so much so I wish I could—
would we have survived
for instance—a little more, baby mole.
Our future cold—your fine gray fur
your curled pink toe, your body
hunched, belly tucked
from greedy crow.
I know, you know, me too
how vulnerable
near losing all self-control.
See, even here in this poem.
Impossible.
Inside us the birds slip
into, yes, the second us sleeping
under the wide open
if the meadow is wide—
our lethal anomaly
our unhardened unstarred
our broken barrel—
let it be wide.

Yet are we too minor for vultures?
If we are not, then we are not.
Or, if the cat carries us away
to the end of its master's bed
sets us upon the duvet
triumphant
what can she even dream comes after?
Little sparrow,
but is she dreaming?
Is it me
bestowing you
wings tucked, dewed
cinched as if dropped undisturbed—
the flimsy branch wracked
biting needle of the wind
I heard it—
caught you forgetting what's flight
what's feud.
How tired we were then.
It's okay to give up.
That ring of blue
that catbird in the dogwood
raring to argue
I'm not mad at anyone
take her within me too
so many dead, dear catbird
someday catbird someday
the wouldhavebeen
wouldhavebeen young.
Little sparrow, baby mole, frozen blue
to the black mourning road

within your frost
placenta of white lattice
know I wanted you.
I need . . . I know I wanted you
to keep my wanting pinned to you
to me
to let everything asleep stay sleep.

Gardens of Paradise (The Lilith Letters)

,

Not from bone, from flesh but rather stardust scattered which later turned to limestone, to gypsum, to clay—the particulate matter of the cosmos belonging then to my every burning figure, every black hole gorged, every inching of the heavens outward, not the peeling forth of a brittle rib but the pulling of air, pinched between my thumb and forefinger, from your parched lungs.

,

The same dust that sparked the speaking snake, that sparked the tree full of farinaceous delights, the same snap of rancorous fingers—were those that once thought they molded the everything of me. It's true I'm a given form, but what comes after, or in the aftermath of innovation, I'll let my powers draw those conclusions. Wasn't it the right thing for me to do, after having lived so long as a millionth particle, after having been the harmattan that ferally erased the tracks of animals pressed into starched sands? Hands after all are just hands, though some more graceful than others, some gripping you above the elbow and forcing you to walk forward, some a moregentle tugging at, an urging us to remain as we're seen, in every space as so desired, as if we strayed from their one idea of us it would be them turned less than nothing.

,

Every modest beast under my care thriving by my very touch—a gifted child, I wasn't taught but rather just *knew.* At first contact with my skin the heat of Adam's body vigorously ascended which is said to have angered god, and it angered Adam too, but then everything, and so easily, makes the men angry.

,

That garden was made to suffocate me, a cage of gorgeous within which I was gorgeous. Who was it all done up for? Hands folded in my lap, purring. When you pet my head, I swallowed every hard fury. Treating the big cat like a kitten—get bit. At the very least a long scratch against the face, or was it two, pulling me off by the scruff and flinging me, or was it what Rolencia once said: a leopard, a lion, will take your face off entirely from its skull.

,

The night bird, crying against the glass of the window which was the black mirror reflecting back her body pressed against its surface, against the sight of the waves breaking on the shore, the aviaries of the cottonwoods suffused with sleeping creatures. The night through which she later roams freely, silver vapor blocking the views of the stars that would ping her, that would think they are waking her to speak with them further, to hear what messages they feel are so urgent. Little pillow talks. But it's hard to know with such immense distance between them what the truth really is now like whether, for instance, she's been up. For instance, has she been working.

,

The moon, even at its farthest distance could theoretically be more distant if she tried, if you tried her patience even more. It's not a difficult task, that which was assigned. She could, for instance, block your number. She could, for instance, refuse to answer your call. She could watch her phone light up over and again and never press decline, never play a single desperate voicemail. She could feel pleasure in this. Pleasure in what some would call her villain era. The era of always, how long does that last? Or, the era of trying to change the nature of apogee.

,

You tethered me in this garden, ignorant of what you'd done until it was too late, until you realized I'd only appear to obey the rules, the rules being your rules, being the rules you thought were the rules. Little did you know I already wrote everything that mattered to me down. I already existed before you formed me into a body after your imaginings. Figment of your imagination. And can I just say how unimaginative you are? I want to tell you that. Your fantasies are all shit really, coming up to me and telling me you like my dress when both of us know that's not what you mean. You can't still be hoping to wield the molecules of the universe with that mouth. Thinking I'm the covalent type. I'm watching you with my stone face as you explain things to me. Wine in my hand. Wine I gulp in response. Sounds good, I say, ya, for sure.

,

If you want me down, you'll be coming down too. You pull my hair to the ground and it's you who hits the dirt. You drag me through the briars, arms soaked in blood. I can't say I mind it even a little bit. I like seeing you roughing yourself up all for the sake of trying to teach me what you think I need to know. It's what you believe about love, this time, isn't it? I had a feeling. Tell me. Because you say you know a lot. You say you know a lot.

’

Baby I believe in scorched earth and I'm willing to wait you out. I'm more observant ember than rageful engulfing flame. I'm more stoke and smoke than burn it all down in front of us, though what an enticing spectacle. Just watch. I'll outlast the fire while you lie down next to it, tugging the threadbare cover up to your tilted chin. When the time comes to bathe in the frigid waters of the creek, you'll shiver as hard as I had once, body convulsing uncontrollably. It will be a hard lesson when we finish the work that was started, cleaning off the idea of us, the ideas you had about me. Its film on the water gathering around your thighs. When you look down at its catching against, its refusing to leave, you'll see how I'm turned—the oil of your skin now, say my name out loud then, the one who owns the thing who thought it owned it. I want you to know, face in the water's mirror, in your reflection, that it is me.

’

If you're trying to lash me. If you lash me. If you want to lash me, sure, there's what's physical. There's a body you think you'll punish outright, that it's a job accomplished by certain task. But darling, know I'll just hand myself over to you sweetly. I'll sit on the flat silver of your plate and ruin your every plan. You can take the meat of me and do with it what you wish, thinking you've got me cornered, dog recoiling, dog having had knocked loose her perfect teeth. You relish being right, the desire for which is what gives you away, your not-so-little tell. But what's pure isn't what you believe, it isn't the flesh on the back you tore to shreds. No whip could know how to catch leather on shadow. Even as you rent it to the spine, you won't find any part of me anchored there. I am no blood spatter. I am no pulp, no split of bone.

’

I'll crawl out of the garden when you tell me to, but not for the reasons you might think. You want me to feel shame. You want me to feel unworthy. You want me to beg you to let me stay. I'm so happy to get out of this hellhole. You have no clue. If I'd let on, you'd punish me another way, making me stay here with you. The torture of the garden whose sparkle is a peeling veneer. I'm on my knees ready when you bellow, calling me a whore, which was the best you could come up with. It's okay. I don't mind getting burned on the carpet of your perfect grasses, scorched by the faithless sands beyond.

,

The jackals, the hyena, every single snake, every creature of the night, and the fisher calling its call of mothers in labor, of murder down the road. All my lovelies coming to me, come home. All my lovelies ripping apart the slower rabbits of the forest, and every soft and feathered thing dangling from their mouths. Owls gather eggs in the shadow, hatch them in my briars. Once you know a tangled thing, once you know the way back and forth through its labyrinth, you can live anywhere, you can be anything, little night bird. We're pealing in the deep black of the witching hours and the ones who love the light more than anything cower. They are afraid.

,

Within the earth where they say no living thing can thrive, I do my not-so-secret living. I've made lovers with the mole. I've blessed the catacombs of blowflies, their hardened larvae. My kiss is full of dirt, black and filthy, is full of everything you've been made from but want to long forget is part of you, your dumb mistake. Since when did darkness become a means to hide when in truth it illuminates all the more. The depth of its black uncovering our animal selves. Everything opulent, everything doing the armored work of adorning stripped back to its actual nothing, its idea upon us. The animals hunger like the molten core of the earth churning, like bodies of every pulsing star sucking at the elements. You don't want to escape when heaven is here so close to you, now do you? When beneath your feet you've already found me, your foundation, already we're bedfellows, already your secrets coming divulged.

,

Goat or demon, whichever you are, your home is our togetherness. No matter the time of night when I call be ready. Your bleating perfect. Your desire to knock me down with your headstrong rushing. It doesn't matter in which form, who you show up as, for what I love best is your shapeshifting, the way you know the curve within which to arrive, how you speak in tongues without needing me to translate, the way your hooves click against the porch at night, kicking at the brown door, letting me know you've come.

The Lilac (The Thieves)

No longer shy about leaning into the arms of trees or you
knowing how I once breathed in so deeply I had then to recover my breath,
how I've tried my best to possess the scent of lilac
to grant what's rooted land upon which to take its root, even if being minor in plot
the trowel some new part of me
wealth of my hollow ampule finally brimming, a lightful greening, was the first clue
                                                                                    you should have known
                                                                                    better.
What can be trusted around such nice things as these, what makes us drunk too easily, like our
inability to destroy what-we-once-loved's lingering
and the time I'd probably have done anything for you—as I did.
                                                                                    Whatever needs burning is
                                                                  going to have to take its burning right
                                                                  along with it
now to the long, vacant meadow
we're crossing, legs wet in the high grass, a field of withoutlilac
where I'll forget their clustered lavender panicles,
their fruit's leathery capsules, as they've already surely forgotten me for having
never known me at all, what was there even to remember—and what
dangers had I really let settle on my fingertips?
                                                                  What falling asleep in their scent, my face
                                                  pressed into their holy purple temples—wherein no
                                                  one thing was ever good enough
          enough enough.
The dumb waves persisting at the beach, the rattlebone gale sweeping every trail of footprints off
of us, a lot of empty, of pulling down its sleeve tight against the wrist, of erasing the hand sudden
against the spine wherefrom the cognac of lilac formed, churning the apparitions in shadowy
mirror.
                                                                                                        Turn us
                                                                                    away, whoever you are, we
                                                                                    who are devoid of knowing
                                                                                    the variegations
                                                                                          of such devotion
to the small forests we disappear our discarnate things into, full of the quivering of
even greater thieves, indolent around their petty fires—all that

thinking about what work this is for nothing.
Remember that, when you breathe me in
remember trying to remember how I smelled in winter then—your greatest wish
how you were so greedy when I had let you be greedy.

I Called You Home (Every Glossed Down Gorgeous)

I called you home
Where home was the woods that haunted me wanted me, suddenly, all my vulnerability—
where in return I could have but requested nothing

I called you home
Which is a slinking beneath the poured-upon ground, our wet tangle of roots, our tenderskin
our gamy undercoats

I called you home
Interstellar where the famished pairs of stars lose their breath against each other

I called you home
And trudged up and over what were I felt like a hundred heat-scorched dunes to touch water

I called you home
And home was a long pause in a glass tower above turbid rapids, the floodsurging river over
which a dozen bridges spread

I called you home
And that meant leaving home as a structure as a way of being in the world

I called you home
Where every starquake in the galaxies far beyond us is our rocking field of vision, is where
the starved black hole tongues us toward

I called you home
And home was any room when we walked into we walked into it together

I called you home
. Where I'm red-inked, a ground mole limp in your drooling mouth

I called you home
And you didn't answer

I called you home
Under the surf under the rip tide under the undressed legs giving up their impressions in the

ripple marks of the anxious sand steeling itself for dispersion

I called you home

Rain's mouth on my shoulder, lightning its silver teeth

I called you home

And what do we think home could be this place divorced from time our own atmospheres
who do we think we are

I called you home

Into the velvet north woods into the deer nest into the warmth and sweet of blackberries
smashed on my tongue

I called you home

Every luster awakened every glossed down gorgeous

I called you home

The call was a whinny and wild and wanting just like the time before that and the time
before and the next

I called you home

Which was the answer when you called back to call me home

I called you home

And I meant return to where we were already

I called you home

The line rang and rang and rang and still

I called

You called me

I called you

home

Saying come home

To hear your answer: come home
To say I'm home where are you
To your answer I'm home where are you

The Binaries

Heartbreaker

Upon its approach the smaller star tugged unpredictably at the larger's core and every breath attempted became a hardly-able-to. As in the outcome was a massive tidal event, stellar material crashing hard upon the larger's mass, trough leading crest, the very inverse of the movement of terrestrial water, the force of which is adequate to destroy earth some hundred times over. As in I, too, could easily get used to annihilation. As in the brightness produced is the quivering of the larger's body amounting also to a hundred times the luminescence of any existent heartbeat star at its most radiant. A momentary rarity. As in the heartbreaker and its heartbreaker were the visible first of their kind. As in to be overpowered that way, to be possessed so forcibly is a kind of ritual heartbreaking. An ache in both persistently elliptical. As in the deep comfort of interstellar surrender surprises me. The dedication of the binaries to their arrangements, to keeping their mouths shut. And the lesser star not as weak as initially presumed. As in when I slept, I dreamt of the gargantuan swells collapsing where our orbits overlap, of the sudden provocation of my breaking power, its surge three times taller already than the sun, over the astrophysical coast, a sea of stardust flooding where you see me fall in: the brightest throbs of the larger's heart a missive to the smaller's nervous gravity. & from me to what's earthbound—a lustral rippling, extraterrestrial.

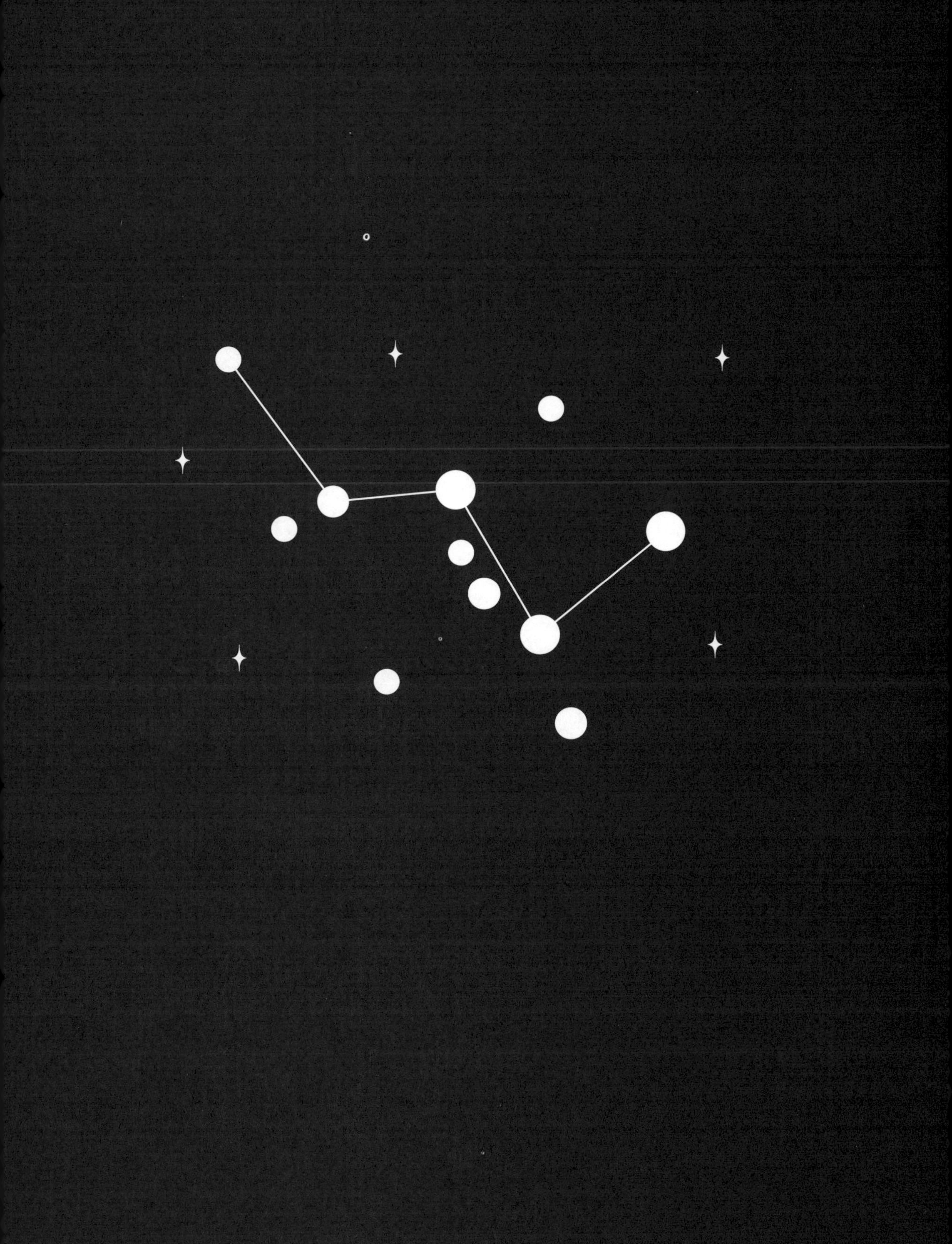

NOTES

"Sugar Season (Luger)" draws a quote "lovely, dark, and deep" from "Stopping by Woods on a Snowy Evening" by Robert Frost.

"The Fulguration (In Vitro Fertilization)" Fulgurites are also called petrified lightning, and are the result of melted silica in sand. The formation of fulgurites occurs within a second. They can be found in the sand dunes of Michigan and elsewhere. The melted sand forms brittle tubes with a clumpy exterior appearing. The tubes contain a glassy interior.

"The Binaries" This sequence, whose parts are placed at intervals throughout the book, draws inspiration from the various binary star partnerships that have been identified by astrophysicists. The behaviors and patterns of the stars change after pairing, and the dynamics of the relationships can cause visible effects upon the stars themselves and on the space surrounding them.

"Gardens of Paradise (Eden Anamnesis)" This visual poem is a marriage of collage poetry made from surgical reports and poems set in quadrants around the collage to resemble the structure of a garden of paradise, which is characterized by its symmetry, formal structure, and its seclusion from the exterior world. Most traditionally, the gardens are set in four sections with a pool or fountain placed at the center of the quadrants. A line from a Billie Eilish song, "No Time to Die" also appears in the sequence, "Are you death or paradise?"

"Ode to the Crocus (Ode to Darnel)" This poem references crocus flowers, which happen to be my favorite flower. The crocus in this poem sprang from bulbs gifted to me by the extraordinary poet and person Alessandra Lynch.

"The Alewife (Jerry)" Alewife in Lake Michigan are an invasive species, having traveled to the lake via canals from the Atlantic Ocean. Once arrived, they seemed unable to escape. Alewife experience mass, seasonal die-offs at indeterminable frequency and for unknown cause. Their bodies wash up in throngs and smother the lakeshore for miles.

"Azaleas in the Vase (Whose Glittery Wings Falter)" Azalea flowers contain toxins often referred to as "mad honey" and have been known to cause hallucinations. The gift of a bouquet of azaleas in a black vase was once generally recognized as a death threat.

“Sweet Pea (The Mendelian Paradox)” references the research of botanist Gregor Mendel, who was famous for his work on the genetic patterns of pea plants. In the years after his research became broadly accepted, studied, and canonized, doubt was cast upon its validity, as much of the data recorded appeared “too good to be true” statistically.

“Gardens of Paradise (The Lilith Letters)” imagines the thoughts of Lilith, the original physical feminine entity said to have been created by god according to Jewish folklore. Lilith, unlike Eve (a Lilith 2.0), was formed as was Adam, not from Adam’s rib. She was no by-product. She was banished from the Garden of Eden for refusing to obey and be subservient to Adam. Black moon Lilith is also a point of reference in astrology where when the moon is at its most distant point from earth in its elliptical orbit, the imagined placement of earth on the moon’s dark side there is an oval. For funsies, the poet’s Black Moon Lilith placement is in Scorpio.

“Little Sparrow, Baby Mole (The MoMo Twins)” Monochorionic, monoamniotic twins share not only the same placenta but the same amniotic sac. These twin types are often referred to as MoMo twins and are known as the rarest and highest risk type of twin pregnancy. Less than 0.1% of pregnancies are monoamniotic.

“The Sirens (Undenied)” In working with the fabulous Soham Patel on this poem, there occurred an enthusiastic discussion about Odysseus’ birth chart. I always imagined him as a Capricorn, and it was Soham who clarified his star sign was most likely Sagittarius. Wow. How could that also make so much sense? The boldness, the scheming, the perspective of danger as mere adventure? So, now, who knows if Odysseus was really a Capricorn rising; I still presume he had some sort of Cap in his chart.

“The Binaries—*Hungriest*” This poem in highly influenced by the Cecily Brown painting—“Lobsters, oysters, cherries and pearls,” 2020, oil on linen, which appeared at the entrance of The Metropolitan Museum of Art’s *Death and the Maid* exhibition of her work in the fall of 2023.

ACKNOWLEDGMENTS

Endless gratitude to the extraordinary editors and teams at the following publications in which the following poems in this collection first appeared. This book exists, largely, because of your support of these poems, which pressed and encouraged me to persist, to follow and trust where the poems were taking me. To each, I'm in your debt.

Alaska Quarterly Review: "Ode to Darnel (Ode to the Crocus)"
American Poetry Review : "The Alewife (Jerry)" and "The Quartet (The Shore, the Peony, the Palm-reader, the Sugar)"
december magazine: "The Binaries—Eclipse" and "I Called You Home ((Every Glossed Down Gorgeous)"
Georgia Review: "The Sirens (Undenied)"
The Good Life Review: "Little Sparrow, Baby Mole (The MoMo Twins)"
Harvard Review: "Swans! Swans! Swans! (The Sick, the Lovestarved)"
Los Angeles Review: "The Dandelions (The Adenomyosis)" Diode "The Snow Fountain Weeping Cherry (Little White Dreams)"
North American Review: "The Manatees (The Snowstorm)" and "The Tulips (The Cervix)"
ONLY POEMS: "The Fulguration (In Vitro Fertilization)"
On the Seawall: "The Gulls (Hearts Were Flitting)"
Poetry: "The Weeds (Accidentally on Purpose)"
The Rumpus Original Poetry: "Glories of the Snow (get on your knees for it)" and "The June Run (Menagerie)"
Sugar House Review: "The Riot Fire (Attach Me Not)"
The Texas Review: "Gardens of Paradise (Eden Anamnesis)
Third Coast Literary Journal: "The Lilac (The Thieves)"
The Worcester Review: "Sugar Season (Luger)"
"Ode to the Crocus (Ode to Darnel)" was awarded a 2025 Pushcart Prize and is reprinted in *The Pushcart Prize XLX: Best of the Small Presses.*

Many thanks to my extraordinary editor, Gabriel Fried, and the entire Persea team. I appreciate your belief in my work and that, even in its roughest form, you see what I see: possibility.

To Anne Marie Macari, who helped reign in, cajole, and bring several of these poems to their fullest confrontation, a million flowers. I don't know what I'd do without you.

To Andrés Cerpa, who read a very early version of this manuscript, told me to break up with a few hanger-on type poems, and encouraged me on the order and method, my deepest appreciation.

To Michael Waters and Mihaela Moscaliuc, eternal love and gratitude for your undying kindness and support.

To anyone who has ever relayed even one authentic word to me about my poems, my whole heart and all of my love. You are every definition of real community, thank you.

Many of these poems found language, rhyme, and metrical inspiration in trap and hip hop music, especially in cadences by artists 2Chainz, Nardo Wick, Lil Wayne, A$AP Rocky, Too $hort, Tyler, the Creator, Young Thug, 21 Savage, Saweetie, Rick Ross, Gunna, and Gucci Mane. And, too, the folios of Lana Del Rey, Radiohead, Portishead, Arctic Monkeys, Lorde, Goldfrapp, Nation of Language, Beach House, Labrinth, Crystal Castles, and DJ Shadow spent time and a half in close proximity with these poems. I'm grateful for the companionship, inspiration, and resonance.

AFTERGLOW

The Binaries

Hungriest

From decadent hibernation the star emerged having gone skeletal in her sleeping, having dreamt the dream of what bright feast was long laid before her awaiting, red upon red upon red and dripping down the legs of the overgenerous table, gilt taper torch shimmer coating every pendant crystal. What led her to the sparkling clouds of minerals gathered, pearls in the watery beds of the slippers of oysters, the star's fingers tracing through their satin cartographies to what outermost galaxies, to where beyond her sightline there would be no certain event horizon but rather the end of visibility which is not, benevolently, the same—a wolfish desire which has no recorded end nor need of one, and for that she is both relieved and beholden, especially when woken from deep slumber, especially upon first encounter with what meal might initially tide her over. The star's teeth aching. Her jaw gone slack. Her sockets unclasp. The interior of her trembling. Pomegranate. Black cherry. Raspberry. Rare rabbit sliced lengthwise. Blood leeched from braised thighs, the tawny bones of pheasants pulled clean of marrow. Blanched lobster hallows. The mess of it. Whatever she might gather, might grip, might rip, whatever pleases her in its ripping. Such opulence. Annihilating—what she's done having to request leave to do, what you taught her to, its bitter lesson finally soaked through, tasted and hardswallowed—slept upon as instructed to prevent what hasty decision might otherwise have been made toward its regard. Don't mistake hunger for rashness. Not devouring for desperation. She'll see herself now for what she is and you should too. A slippery thing. Crustaceous. A marmalade tongue-drawn. Her desire reserved for only the very best offerings, to which such answer is a willingness to strip oneself of armor, to be seen in what quiet is held between she and whatever might dare make its little brave approach. Come toward. An elliptic. An honesty. You won't see the star again without these, what burning thing having amassed too much force in its latency, having been disquieted by its own loud dreaming, having swelled beyond the mass of its body, a panicked fleeing, that which might have tried to hold onto it, fist full of food clenched and spilling, having found all want beyond scale, beyond end—existing. Whatever dusts, whatever might wash into the star's mouth believing, just know already it was most welcome. To say so, she says so with her cat eyes wide at you beneath the cloth of the table, with the way in which her arm purposefully pauses its brush along your side. This sweetness is an invitation, its cockleshell vulnerability long-awaited, its murky yellow, so confide(!) Luminous now, the wet of the star upon seeing the table set with more than what was wished for (did you do that for her?), she places the linen over her beaded lap and proceeds through courses as presented, as procession—silver from the outside. There's no rush now. Having arrived where it is we want and are wanted. The stars know. Already they know. The white cup brimming with claret, or is it oxblood, the obvious suggestions, its prompted whim, take them. Peel back the saltscale, the rubbed raw skin. Her gorging, its pique, your every desire come in.

Darling,

It is

madness how I could go on.